"Bringing to bear his expertise in law and theology, George Gatgounis provides a welcome and refreshing study of John Calvin's understanding and use of law. After viewing Calvin's legal theory and political theory, the author shows the outworking of these in Geneva as well as surveying how Calvin's views aligned compared with other reformers in the same theological tradition. There is much to be learned from this unique book."

—**Timothy J. Demy**
Professor of Military Ethics, U. S. Naval War College

"Calvin was not only a theologian but trained in law, as Dr. Gatgounis and I have been, and this influenced the manner in which he approached the study of theology and his interest in theology's influence upon law and government. I found George's work insightful and balanced. His work is well worth reading more than once. I heartedly endorse the book."

—**H. Wayne House**
Distinguished Research Professor of Theology, Law, and Culture, Faith International University and Faith Seminary

"While Calvin is remembered chiefly as a reformer, Gatgounis demonstrates the organic connection between his theology and his jurisprudence as well as their collaborative force in sixteenth-century Geneva, where Puritan zeal sought to transform church and state. This well-researched volume also charts Calvin's influence in colonial New England."

—**Charles L. Echols**
Adjunct Professor, Cummins Memorial Theological Seminary

CALVIN THE MAGISTRATE

CALVIN THE MAGISTRATE

His Political and Legal Legacy

Religion and Law Series, Volume One

George J. Gatgounis

WIPF & STOCK · Eugene, Oregon

CALVIN THE MAGISTRATE
His Political and Legal Legacy

Religion and Law Series, Volume One

Copyright © 2021 George J. Gatgounis. All rights reserved. Except for brief quotations in critical publications or reviews, no part of this book may be reproduced in any manner without prior written permission from the publisher. Write: Permissions, Wipf and Stock Publishers, 199 W. 8th Ave., Suite 3, Eugene, OR 97401.

Wipf & Stock
An Imprint of Wipf and Stock Publishers
199 W. 8th Ave., Suite 3
Eugene, OR 97401

www.wipfandstock.com

PAPERBACK ISBN: 978-1-7252-6117-4
HARDCOVER ISBN: 978-1-7252-6116-7
EBOOK ISBN: 978-1-7252-6118-1

JANUARY 28, 2021

CONTENTS

CALVIN THE MAGISTRATE: THE LEGAL AND POLITICAL LEGACY OF THE GENEVAN REFORMER | 1

INTRODUCTION | 3
   John Calvin | 3
   John Calvin—the Religious & Political Landscape
     of His Day | 8
   Conclusion | 14
   Statement of Thesis | 14

THE LEGAL THEORY OF JOHN CALVIN | 15
   Calvin's View of the Uses of the Law | 15
   Calvin's View of the Source of Law | 18
   Calvin's View of the Relation of Law and the Gospel | 20
     The Distinction Between Law and Grace | 20
     The Continuity of Law and Gospel | 21
   Calvin's View of the Prosecutorial Function of Law | 23
   Conclusion | 24

THE POLITICAL THEORY OF JOHN CALVIN | 25
   Calvin's Theory of Church and State | 26
   Calvin's Theory of Checks and Balances
     on Political Power | 30
   Calvin's Theory of the Citizen's Relation to Government | 38
   Calvin's Theory of the Relation of Government to God | 44
   Conclusion | 45

THE ROLE OF THE CONSISTORY AT GENEVA | 46
  Economic Strictures | 47
  Examples of Social Infractions | 48
  Examples of Sanctions | 49
  Conclusion | 50

COMMON POLITICAL THEMES AMONG CALVIN'S
FELLOW REFORMERS | 51
  Various Lutherans | 51
  Francis Turretin | 51
  Peter Martyr Vermigli | 52
    Theodore Beza | 54
  Johannes Phillipe du Plessis-Mornay | 54
  Johannes Cocceius | 56
  Johannes Cloppenburg | 59
  William Ames | 60
  John Goodwin | 62
  Samuel Rutherford | 63
  John Owen and John Locke | 66
  John Knox | 67
    Knox's Spiritual Development, the Reformation in Scotland, and
      Knox's Questions About Its Course | 67
    The Sources of Knox's Political Theology | 69
    The Common Views of Knox, Goodman, and Ponet | 70
    Knox's Own Summary of His Political Theology | 73
  Conclusion | 74

CONCLUSION | 75

CALVIN'S MAGISTERIAL INFLUENCE EXTENDED
THROUGH PURITANISM—AN OVERVIEW OF PURITAN
JURISPRUDENCE | 76
  The Teleology of Puritan Jurisprudence | 77
    The Vision of a National Puritan Utopia | 78
    Sabbath Observance—The Crux of Puritan Social Theory | 79
    The Centrality of Preaching in Puritanism | 82

Excursus—Congregationalist Puritan Jurisprudence in Practice in New England | 84
    Substantive Puritan Law | 84
    The Cohesive Social Order Established by Puritan Law | 88
    A Portait of a Victim of Puritan Jurisprudence:
        Obadiah Holmes | 89
The Relation of Puritan Covenant Theology and the Puritan Sociology | 91
The Influence of the Puritan War With Charles and the Prelates on Puritan Legal Theory | 92
The Puritan Ideology of Church and State | 95
    Cartwright's Teaching of the Distinction of the Church and
        State | 96
    Cartwright's Teaching on the Relation Between Church
        and State | 99
    Cartwright's Teaching on the Nature of Church Government
        and State Government | 102
Conclusion | 104

A FOCUS ON PROCEDURAL LAW IN THE CALVINISTIC REFORMATION IN NEW ENGLAND—THE ROLE OF JUDGE SAMUEL SEWALL IN THE SALEM WITCH TRIALS | 105
    Introduction: The Manner and Content of Sewall's Public Confession in the Witch Trials | 106
        The "How" of the Confession—The Manner of Sewall's
            Recanting | 106
        The "What" of the Confession—The Written Recantation | 106
    ANALYSIS: THE "WHY" OF THE CONFESSION—
    SEWALL'S MOTIVATION | 107
        The "Who" of the Confession—Sewall's Psychological, Moral, and
            Religious Underpinnings | 108
        His Critics and His Character | 108
        His Temperament | 109
        His View of the Value of Human Life | 110
        His Epitaph | 113

The *"Why" of the Confession—The Function of Sewall's Perception of Religious Law* | 114
  Substantive Puritan Law | 115
  The Cohesive New England Social Order | 116
The *"In Re" of the Confession—The Tragic Superstitions* | 118
The *"In Re" of the Confession—Group Hysteria* | 120
The *"In Re" of the Confession—Mock Examination of Witnesses* | 122
The *"In Re" of the Confession—The Barbaric Torture* | 125
The *"In Re" of the Confession—The Possible Gender Factor* | 128
CONCLUSION: THE INTERPLAY OF RELIGIOUS, MORAL, AND PSYCHOLOGICAL FACTORS | 129

CONCLUSION: THE LEGACY OF THE LEGAL AND POLITICAL THEORY OF JOHN CALVIN | 132
  Calvin's Expansive and Extensive Influence | 133
  Calvin Was an Amalgam of the Influences of His Day | 133
  The Excursus on the Salem Witch Trials Illustrates a Gaping Hole of Lack of Reform in the Law of Evidence | 134
  Religious Toleration and Pluralism Were Not on the Radar in Calvin's Day | 135
  Calvin's Driving Purpose Was the Question of His Time | 135

BIBLIOGRAPHY | 137
INDEX OF SCRIPTURE | 139
INDEX OF SUBJECTS | 145

CALVIN THE MAGISTRATE
The Legal and Political Legacy of the Genevan Reformer

It is only fitting that my good friend and fellow author-theologian Dr. George Gatgounis chose John Calvin's legal and political legacy as this remarkable book's subject. As it was with Calvin, Dr. Gatgounis' calling finds him firmly planted in the midst of that sometimes complicated place where theology, law, and politics intersect. Also in similarity to Calvin, Dr. Gatgounis is not merely a brilliant subject-matter expert but also a catalyst for change—he, like Calvin, is a reformer with an unfettered devotion to God and an unparalleled conviction to do what is right in God's eyes. This book is borne of that conviction, and it is as vitally important as it is relevant.

Just before Dr. Gatgounis went to Harvard, the Soviet empire collapsed. In response to the many fledgling democracies that quickly arose from the rubble, the Kennedy School at Harvard set aside $6 million to fund a think tank to answer the question "What makes democracies work?" As it is with so many puzzling and awe-inspiring events of our time, contemporary understanding is revealed through an exploration of historical events. This work is the product of the author's own perpetually full think tank, providing the answer to Harvard's literal $6 million question through the example of sixteenth-century Geneva, a democracy which literally sprang up overnight to form a functioning republic.

CALVIN THE MAGISTRATE

Since the fall of the Soviet Union, other empires have fallen, and as so many emergent democracies stand precariously on wobbly newborn legs, their best protection against failure lies within our own understanding of an elective government's formation, foundation, and fundamental development. Our comprehension of these matters becomes even more vital in light of our nation's increased involvement in the advancement of representative governments throughout the world, and it is for this reason this book becomes necessary reading.

The content contained within this study is remarkable in its precision, and the vivid and detailed picture it provides regarding the ideas, attitudes, and philosophies of Calvin's Geneva is one only achieved through exhaustive research and painstaking analysis. Even so, while the comprehensive nature of this work's exposition is awe-inspiring in and of itself, this book's real treasure is gained through the author's profound insight into human character—since after all, it is by and through a nation's people that a democratic government is built and sustained.

To this end, Dr. Gatgounis paints a portrait of John Calvin that is so well-researched and well-rounded that he seems to jump from the book's very pages. It is with great objectivity, integrity, even-handedness, and compassion that the author presents us with a complete perspective of Calvin, as a magistrate and as a man who is overcome by yearning for righteousness to earn God's favor, through and despite his frailty and flaws. No longer incarcerated by the dusty iron chains of history, Dr. Gatgounis' Calvin is alive, relevant, relatable, and most importantly and impressively—he is human.

H. Wayne House

INTRODUCTION

JOHN CALVIN

We know of Calvin from his enemies as well as from his followers—Pope Pius IV says of him, "The strength of that heretic consisted in this, that money never had the slightest charm for him. If I had such servants my dominion would extend from sea to sea."[1] John Cotton, an American Puritan who admired Calvin: "I have read the fathers and the school men, and Calvin too; but I find that he that has Calvin has them all."[2] When Cotten was asked why he studied into the small hours more than he had previously, he replies, "Because I love to sweeten my mouth with a piece of Calvin before I go to sleep."[3] Some detractors of Calvin regard such admiration of Calvin's works as idolatry, but these naysayers notwithstanding, his works are impossible to ignore.[4]

We can learn much of Calvin from his opponents:

---

1. Otto Scott, "The Great Christian Revolution," in *The Great Christian Revolution—The Myths of Paganism and Arminianism* (Vallecito, Calif.: Ross House Books, 1991), p. 130.

2. Cotton Mather, *Magnalia Christi Americana* (Hartford, 1853), I, p. 274.

3. Mather, I, p. 274.

4. One seminarian at a large conservative Protestant seminary heard a Calvinistic student cite a section of Calvin's *Institutes*. The seminarian remarked in rebuke, alluding to the Apostle Paul at Mars Hill (Acts 17:1ff.), "I came to the shrine of the unknown god, whose name was Calvin." The seminarian proposed that all Calvinists were actually idolaters who deify the Swiss Reformer.

Calvin has, I believe, caused untold millions of souls to be damned.[5]

If Calvin ever wrote anything in favor of religious liberty, it was a typographical error.[6]

It was the fact that Calvin's own character was compulsive-neurotic which transformed the God of Love as experienced and taught by Jesus into a compulsive character, bearing absolutely diabolical traits in his reprobatory practice.[7]

But we shall always find it hard to love the man who darkened the human soul with the most absurd and blasphemous conception of God in all the long and honored history of nonsense.[8]

Historians tend to ignore, however, that Calvin was often ill, especially in his later life, with a collection of maladies, duly reported to physicians at Montpelier the year of his death, which included acute symptoms such as kidney stones, pulmonary tuberculosis, quartan fever, intestinal parasites, thrombosed hemorrhoids, and a spastic colon.[9]

The biographer Susanne Selinger sees Calvin as neurotic, a man whose neurosis emerges in remarks about the human body in a bitter belligerence, and censoriousness directed at anti-social behavior, especially of a sexual kind. Selinger sees Calvin as Jung's "the introverted thinker." The type is awkward in expressing emotion and ill at ease with public attention. Selinger contends that

5. As quoted by Edwin H. Palmer, *The Five Points of Calvinism* (Grand Rapids: Baker Book House, 1980), p. 26.

6. As quoted by Gordon H. Clark, *Predestination* (Phillipsburg: Presbyterian and Reformed Publishing Co., 1987), p. 144.

7. William G. T. Shedd, *Calvinism: Pure and Mixed* (Edinburgh: Banner of Truth Trust, 1986), p. xviii.

8. As quoted by William G.T. Shedd, *Calvinism: Pure and Mixed* (Edinburgh: Banner of Truth Trust, 1986), p. 149.

9. W. Fred Graham, "Calvin and the Political Order: An Analysis of the Three Explanatory Studies," in R.V. Schnucker, ed., *Calviana: Ideas and Influence of Jean Calvin* (Kirksville, Ms.: Sixteenth Century Journal Publishers, 1988), p. 57 n. 17.

INTRODUCTION

Calvin was oedipally ambivalent, since the loss of his mother while a youth was complicated by his father's speedy remarriage. Calvin suppressed feelings of betrayal, Selinger adds, that festered into a passionate hatred, a yearning for love, envy, anger, and fear. These emotions, which could not find expression because of Calvin's religiously oppressive mental regimen, surfaced in his written and spoken works.[10] Bouwsma, another biographer, agrees with Selinger that Calvin's coldness and aloofness toward his father resulted in Calvin's seeking parental figures among the community of Geneva, particularly in the consistory.[11]

Those who have admired Calvin include Charles Haddon Spurgeon, perhaps the most popular English preacher of the nineteenth century, who remarked, "the longer I live the clearer does it appear that John Calvin's system is the nearest to perfection,"[12] adding that "there is no such thing as preaching Christ and him crucified, unless you preach what now-a-days is called Calvinism. I have my own ideas, and those I always state boldly. It is a nickname to call it Calvinism; Calvinism is the Gospel, and nothing else."[13] Even Calvin's enemies would concede his rhetorical superiority: "Calvin . . . was a master of equivocation. His work possessed the great political virtue of ambiguity. It was subject not so much to a private process of internalization and emotional recapitulation, as to a public process of development, accretion, distortion, and use."[14] Had Calvin not been so gifted rhetorically, he would have had fewer enemies because people would have ignored him.

Some even compare Calvin to Paul and Augustine:

---

10. Susanne Selinger, *Calvin Against Himself—An Inquiry in Intellectual History* (Hamden, Conn.: Archon, 1984), p. 62.

11. William J. Bouwsma, *John Calvin: A Sixteenth-Century Portrait* (New York: Oxford University, 1988), p. 113.

12. Charles H. Spurgeon, *Spurgeon's Sovereign Grace Sermons* (Edmonton: Still Waters Revival Books, 1990), p. 18.

13. Charles H. Spurgeon, *Spurgeon's Sovereign Grace Sermons* (Edmonton: Still Waters Revival Books, 1990), p. 129; Phillip Schaff, *History of the Christian Church* (Grand Rapids: William B. Eerdmans, 1910), Vol. 3, p. 486.

14. Michael Walzer, *The Revolution of the Saints: A Study in the Origins of Radical Politicals* (Cambridge, Mass.: Harvard University Press, 1965), p. 23.

Next to Paul, John Calvin has done the most for the world. These two extraordinarily gifted men tower like pyramids over the scene of history.[15]

Calvin easily ranks as one of the outstanding systematic expounders of the Christian system since Saint Paul.[16]

Calvin brought to light forgotten doctrine of the Apostle Paul.[17]

Calvin and Augustine easily rank as the two outstanding systematic expounders of the Christian system since Saint Paul.[18]

Augustine stands as a major link between Paul and Calvin.[19]

[They are] the two most scientific theologians of Christendom.[20]

The main features of Calvin's theology are found in the writings of Saint Augustine.[21]

Augustine was so strongly Calvinistic, that John Calvin referred to himself as an Augustinian theologian.[22]

---

15. Charles H. Spurgeon, *Spurgeon's Sovereign Grace Sermons* (Edmonton: Still Waters Revival Books, 1990), p. 129.

16. Kenneth G. Talbot and W. Gary Crampton, *Calvinism, Hyper-Calvinism, and Arminianism* (Edmonton: Still Waters Revival Books, 1990), p. 78.

17. Loraine Boettner, *The Reformed Doctrine of Predestination* (Phillipsburg: Presbyterian and Reformed Publishing Co., 1932), p. 352.

18. Alan Richardson and John S. Bowden, *The Westminster Dictionary of Christian Theology*, (Philadelphia: Westminster Press, 1983), p. 58.

19. Arthur Custance, *The Sovereignty of Grace* (Philipsburg: Presbyterian and Reformed Publishing Co., 1979), p. 20.

20. Roger Forster and Paul Marston, *Reason and Faith* (Eastbound, Monarch, 1989), p. 272; see also Roger Forster and Paul Marston, *God's Strategy in Human History* (Crowborough, East Sussex: Highland, 1989).

21. Charles D. Provane, *The Bible and Birth Control* (Monongahela: Zimmer Printing House, 1989), p. 68.

22. Provane, p. 97.

INTRODUCTION

> There is hardly a doctrine of Calvin that does not bear the marks of Augustine's influence.[23]
>
> The system of doctrine taught by Calvin is just the Augustinianism common to the whole body of the Reformers.[24]
>
> Calvin got his Calvinism from Augustine.[25]
>
> The reformation was essentially a revival of Augustinianism, as Augustinianism was a recovery of Pauline theology.[26]

Later theologians would praise "Calvinism" as the alternative to "Arminianism." In Reformed circles, since the Reformation, the term Arminianism is the byword for aberration, the common term for all theological evils. Arminianism says that mankind, though fallen, has some moral good. This potential for moral good ranges from the doctrine of free will to the doctrine of the "spark of divinity."[27] Morton Smith calls Arminianism "a crooked stick" through which God can still save.[28] Sam Storms defends Calvinism as the only worthwhile system of salvation doctrine because the alternative, or Arminianism, is "by necessity synergistic, in that it conceives of salvation as the joint or mutual effort of both God

---

23. John Walvoord, *The Millennial Kingdom* (Grand Rapids: Zondervan Publishing House, 1959), p. 19.

24. Provane, p. 49.

25. Provane. p. 49.

26. Arthur Custance, *The Sovereignty of Grace* (Philipsburg: Presbyterian and Reformed Publishing Co., 1979), p. 27.

27. Scholastic theologians distinguish moral good from metaphysical good. According to them, there is metaphysical good even in Satan, although no moral good. Scholastic theologians theorize that God created all things good (Gen. 1:24). Further, they see evil as the absence of good. Since Satan, one third of the angels, as well as Adam and Eve, fell into moral evil yet still exist, they must have some kind of "good." The goodness retained by the fallen beings is metaphysical good. Since these beings lack moral good, they are evil. The Reformed branch of Protestantism has argued since the Reformation that mankind is evil morally but not metaphysically.

28. Morton H. Smith, *Reformed Evangelism* (Clinton: Multi-communication Ministries, 1989), p. 29.

and man."²⁹ "Calvinism stands today as the great citadel of historic orthodoxy."³⁰ J. Gresham Machen, founder of Westminster Theological Seminary, recommended Boetnner's work *The Reformed Doctrine of Predestination*, a work generally considered to define the parameters of Calvinism.³¹ Here R.C. Sproul represents the opinion of Reformed theologians:

> Those thinkers who are most widely recognized as the titans of classical Christian scholarship fall heavily on the Reformed side. I am persuaded, however, that this is a fact of history that dare not be ignored. To be sure, it is possible that Augustine, Aquinas, Luther, Calvin, and Edwards could all be wrong on this matter. Again, that these agreed does not prove the case for predestination. They could have been wrong. But it does get attention."³²

JOHN CALVIN—THE RELIGIOUS & POLITICAL LANDSCAPE OF HIS DAY

A variety of forces shaped Calvin's world (1509-64)—Renaissance humanism, the printing press, Lutheran reform, the reform of the 1520s in France, as well as the more radical aftermath a decade later. Calvin, who made his reputation as a Reformed theologian, was first of all a humanist scholar. (The term connotes the Renaissance rediscovery of the classical form of Greece and Rome.) The humanist caption *ad fontes*, or "back to the original sources," was taken up by the young Calvin; interestingly, his first work was a commentary on Seneca. Not only did humanist scholarship include Latin, Greek, and Hebrew documents, but also the writings of the Church Fathers. Calvin's interests led him to Augustine.

---

29. Samuel C. Storms, *Chosen for Life* (Grand Rapids: Baker Book House, 1987), p. 30.

30. Gregg Singer, *John Calvin: His Roots and Fruits* (Atlanta: A Press, 1989), p. 28.

31. J. Gresham Machen, *The Christian View of Man* (Grand Rapids: Wm. B. Eerdmans Publishing Co., 1931), p. 51.

32. R.C. Sproul, *Chosen by God* (Wheaton: Tyndale House, 1986), p. 15.

INTRODUCTION

Moreover, humanist traditions revived the art of rhetoric, the skillful use of language for persuasion, and this John Calvin used to great advantage.[33]

The advent of the printing press magnified humanist scholarship, taking it far and wide, to audiences hitherto unimagined. Literacy was on the rise, stirred by the publications, the pamphlets and the other printed works in the vernacular. Further, the publication of a barrage of pamphlets in the language of the people actually stirred interest in literacy. Scripture translated into the language of the people had emerged under Hus and Wyclif, but under Luther and Calvin the rediscovery was broadcast to the peoples of Europe and beyond. Indeed, the printing press was the principal weapon of the Reformation. In some parts of Europe, even the power of the Papacy could not overcome the power of the press.[34]

Calvin, a man of his day, became integral to the reform movements that dominated Western Europe. These included both magisterial and radical elements (*magisterial* refers to the position of reformers in regard to government). It was the magisterial branches of the Reformation that advocated use of governments, especially local governments, for the correction of both church and society. The radical branches of the Reformation included anabaptists and spiritualists, who viewed the state (national and

---

33. *Cf.* William G. Naphy, *Calvin and the Consolidation of the Genevan Reformation* (Manchester, New York: Manchester University Press, 1994); Daniel Buscarlet, *International Monument of Reformation: A Short Outline* (Genieve: Editions l'Eau Vive, 196-); *Monument International de la Reformation a Geneve* (Geneve, Imprimerie Atar, 1909?); Henri Naef, *Les origines dal refomea Geneve, la cit'e des 'ev'eques, l'humanimse, les signes preecurseurs; publie par la Societe d'histoire et d'archeologie de geneve, avec le concours de la Socieate auxiliarie des sceince et des arts* (Paris, E. Droz, Geneve, A. Jullien, 1936); for a helpful bibliography, see Theophile Dufour, *Notice Bibliographique sur le Catechisme et la Confession de foi de Calvin (1537) et sur les autres livres imprimes a Geneve et a Neuchatel dans les priemers temps de la Reforme (1533-40)* (Geneve: Slatkine Reprints, 1970).

34. *Cf.* Alister E. McGrath, *A Life of John Calvin* (Oxford, 1990) and Ronald S. Wallace, *Calvin, Geneva, and the Reformation* (Edinburgh, 1989).

local) as arms of Satan. (The Mennonites, Hutterites, and Amish are its modern equivalents.)[35]

In terms of doctrinal influence, Martin Luther propelled Calvin toward Reformation theology. Introspective, and in the thrall of a single question ("how can sinful human beings be justified before a God who is absolutely righteous?"), Luther rejected the responses of the medieval theologians. Because of his own sense of sin in light of God's righteousness, Luther concluded (from the Book of Romans) that God imputed righteousness to unrighteous sinners *sola fide* and *sola gratia*—by grace and by faith alone, and that the only source of religious authority was Scripture. *Sola fide, sola gratia,* and *sola Scriptura* were the inspiration for Calvin's spiritual journey, leading him from Luther to horizons of his own making.[36]

Just as Luther contributed to Calvin's spiritual quest, so did Zwingli, during the formative years. Preaching in Zurich, Zwingli had come to his conclusions independent of Luther. Although both maintained friendly relations until the 1520s, in 1525 they hatched a bitter disagreement over an interpretation of the Lord's Supper, particularly the nature of Christ's presence in the rite. Despite the disagreement, Zwingli contributed to Calvin's development. Calvin's reformist zeal had two birthplaces—Switzerland and Germany, not merely one.[37]

A reform movement also swept through France in the early sixteenth century. A humanist scholar who explored Scripture, Jacques Lefevre D'Etaples epitomized the principle of *sola scriptura*, a ministry that included the writing of biblical commentaries and an attempt to reconstruct the apostolic church. Among the disciples of Jacque Lefevre d'Etaples were John Calvin and Guon Brigomet. Under the ministry of Brigomet, William Farel became

---

35. *Cf.* Alister E. McGrath, *A Life of John Calvin* (Oxford, 1990) and Ronald S. Wallace, *Calvin, Geneva, and the Reformation* (Edinburgh, 1989).

36. *Cf.* Alister E. McGrath, *A Life of John Calvin* (Oxford, 1990) and Ronald S. Wallace, *Calvin, Geneva, and the Reformation* (Edinburgh, 1989).

37. *Cf.* Alister E. McGrath, *A Life of John Calvin* (Oxford, 1990) and Ronald S. Wallace, *Calvin, Geneva, and the Reformation* (Edinburgh, 1989).

INTRODUCTION

a Protestant. Unlike Lefevre, who never advocated a break from Rome, Farel concluded that a break from Rome was imperative if one were to pursue reform to conclusion. Farel and Calvin later joined in Geneva to spread the work of reform throughout Switzerland.[38]

Farel was dissatisfied with Lefevre's reforms, producing the first Protestant writings in the French language. Published in 1524, Farel's commentary on the Lord's Prayer was the first systematic exposition of Protestant theology by a French theologian. The publisher of Farel's work, Pierre de Vingle, began to print additional literature at Neufchatel, advocating more radical reform, including the abrogation of Rome's authority. This culminated in the events of October 17, 1534, when anti-Catholic slogans were placarded all over Paris, including the king's bedchamber. Until then Francis had been open to more moderate attempts at reform, such as LeFevere's. The reaction to the placard campaign, however, was persecution of the more evangelically minded; these included John Calvin. One year after the placard campaign, Calvin, who had fled to Geneva from his native France, would publish his first edition of the *Institutes* in 1536.[39]

From 1530 onward, in France and Geneva, in the Netherlands and in Germany, the reformation reached an epic dimension. In France for instance, the reaction was public burnings, among these the martyrdom of Carolus de Koninck:

> When the priests saw that they could do nothing with him he was condemned as a heretic, and after that, on 22 April degraded from the popish priesthood. Then the bishop delivered him into the hands of the secular judges, just as Christ was given over to the heathen by the priests and the scribes.[40]

---

38. *Cf.* Alister E. McGrath, *A Life of John Calvin* (Oxford, 1990) and Ronald S. Wallace, *Calvin, Geneva, and the Reformation* (Edinburgh, 1989).

39. *Cf.* Alister E. McGrath, *A Life of John Calvin* (Oxford, 1990) and Ronald S. Wallace, *Calvin, Geneva, and the Reformation* (Edinburgh, 1989).

40. Alastair Duke, trans. and ed., "The Seed of the Church—Martyr's Testimonies," *Calvinism in Europe 1540-1610—A Collection of Documents* (Manchester: Manchester University Press, 1992), p. 138.

CALVIN THE MAGISTRATE

In Geneva, the Reformation dismantled the bishopric. In the Genevan diocese (110 parishes under the Catholic bishop), sale of church land between September 1536 and February 1537 raised 47,000 francs, or almost three times the annual revenues of the city. Until then temporal power of the Bishop had been extensive—he received two thirds of the commercial tariffs on Geneva's public markets and all the revenues from the criminal justice system.[41]

Energized by this economic coup, Genevan society was eventually reorganized according to Calvin's vision, and this was derived from biblical sources. Calvin's creation of four offices within the church was to be the organizational structure of society. Under this arrangement, pastors, elders, deacons, and doctors divided responsibilities, respectively, into preaching, discipline, money and material benevolence, as well as teaching.[42]

Not only in France and Geneva, but also in the Netherlands, the reformation surged ever higher, to the extent that in 1578 the Synod of Dordrecht asked whether civil government should confirm or enforce the articles passed by Reformed synods. The Dordrecht Synod, composed of ministers and at least one elder from each assembly, replied "that the civil authority shall be asked to confirm with their authority those articles, where the authority of the same is necessary for these to be put into effect." Thus, if creedal or confessional statements implicated civil authority, the civil government's responsibility was to enforce the decrees of the Reformed synods.[43]

The Reformation ignited in the Netherlands on August 10, 1566, when over 400 cathedrals were vandalized in Flanders alone in seventeen provinces. Well-organized mobs systematically looted, smashed idols, and desecrated church buildings. Although

---

41. William G. Naphy, "The Renovation of the Ministry in Geneva," in *The Reformation of the Parishes* (Manchester: Manchester University Press, 1993), p. 114.

42. Jeannine E. Olson, *Calvin and Social Welfare—Deacons and the Bourse Francaise* (London and Toronto: Associated University Press, 1989), p. 29.

43. Alastair Duke, trans. and ed., "The Synod of Dordrecht, 1578," *Calvinism in Europe 1540-1610—A Collection of Documents* (Manchester: Manchester University Press, 1992), p. 182.

INTRODUCTION

Philip II of Spain, under the Duke of Alva, sent 10,000 troops to suppress "rebellion and heresy," the incursion of foreign "idolatrous" troops only served to inflame the trend.[44]

In Germany, an awareness of God according to Protestant dictates found its way into the coin of the realm—another reflection of expanding Reformation influence. This sense of the superiority of Scripture was a hallmark. Frederick the Wise, host of the Wittenberg "ecclesiastical experiments" (the Wittenberg Movement), issued coins stamped with V[erbum] D[omini] m[anet] i[n] e[ternum].[45]

Robert Kingdon's works on Calvinism identify Geneva as a center of the Reformation and concurrent political revolution.[46] The preaching itself often led to social upheaval, of the most iconoclastic kind. In 1560, the first French riots occurred in Rouen and La Rochelle. A year later in 1561, the furor spread to a host of other French cities, towns and villages, including the province of Languedoc, Paris, Touraine, Angers, Beauvais, LeMans, and Pointoise. By the next year in 1562, riots erupted in Orleans, Tours, Caen, Lyons, Marseille, Abbeville, Bourges, Meaux, Sens, Bayeaux, and Auxerre.[47] In France, unlike Switzerland and Germany, the destruction of a community's "idols" was a direct affront to the King, whose political agenda was "one king, one law, and one faith."[48]

---

44. P. Mack Crew, *Calvinist Preaching and Iconoclasm in the Netherlands* (Cambridge University Press, 1978); Carlos M.N. Eire, *War Against the Idols—The Reformation of Worship from Erasmus to Calvin* (Cambridge: Cambridge University Press, 1986), p. 280.

45. Helga Robinson-Hammerstein, "Introduction: Luther and the Laity," in *The Transmission in the Lutheran Reformation* (Dublin: Irish Academic Press, 1989), p. 29.

46. Robert Kingdon, *Geneva and the Coming of the Wars of Religion in France, 1555-1563* (Geneva, 1956); Robert Kingdon, *Geneva and the Constitution of the French Protestant Movement 1564-1572* (Madison, Wisc., 1967); cf. John T. McNeill, *The History and Character of Calvinism* (New York, 1967), pp. 237-352; E. William Monter, *Calvin's Geneva* (New York, 1975), pp. 165-236.

47. Carlos M.N. Eire, *War Against the Idols—The Reformation of Worship from Erasmus to Calvin* (Cambridge: Cambridge University Press, 1986), p. 279.

48. Carlos M.N. Eire, *War Against the Idols—The Reformation of Worship*

Over time France would prove to be more than fallow ground. The upheavals, however, were not at the instigation of the Genevan consistory; on the contrary, Calvin condemned the riots as sin and a crime.[49]

CONCLUSION

The legal and political scenario of Calvin's day involved upheavals deriving from the force of religion upon law. Whole cities, provinces, and states came under Reformation influence, ranging from quiet individual conversions to Protestantism to the hysteria of community iconoclasm. The transformation of these societies, however, was not moving away from a religious worldview; rather, the transformation was a movement of one religion to another. In Calvin's day, secularism, pluralism, and religious toleration were non-existent. Europe was not in the thrall of the question "Should religion in public life be tolerated?" but rather "Which religion should be enforced, to the banning of all others?"

Calvin was a driven man, but a valid question drove him: *"What is the true religion?"* And deriving from the central question were corollaries: "What law is right law?" and "What government is right government?" Calvin's trek would lead him to answers.

STATEMENT OF THESIS

Calvin concluded that, substantively, a correct political and legal system derives from the Bible, and procedurally, the system is applied by democratically elected officials, checking and balancing one another—and his views were consistent with a Reformation consensus.

---

from Erasmus to Calvin (Cambridge: Cambridge University Press, 1986), p. 281.

49. Eire, p. 280.

THE LEGAL THEORY OF JOHN CALVIN

From a variety of perspectives, law was a principal concern of Reformers. Divine law exposes the personal human need of salvation—because none can perfectly keep divine law, salvation must come in Christ by grace through faith alone. Further, the magisterial branch of the Reformation viewed civil law, as informed by divine law, as a means to reform society. Also, Reformers viewed divine law as a blueprint for practical Christian living. Calvin agreed with his Reformation colleagues that divine law functions as a spiritual teacher, restrainer of sin in society, and a guide to sanctification, yet emphasized the law's divine source, relation to the Gospel, and prosecutorial role.

CALVIN'S VIEW OF THE USES OF THE LAW

The Reformation developed a rough consensus regarding the functions of the law of God, concluding that the first use of the law is tutelary. Regarding this function Calvin cites Romans 10:4, "For Christ is the end of the law."[1] The law acts negatively to expose sin and positively to expose the solution—in the person and finished work of Christ. The second use of the law is its civil function,

---

1. John Calvin, *Calvin: Institutes of the Christian Religion*, 2 vols., ed. John T. McNeill and tr. Ford Lewis Battles, *Library of Christian Classics 20-21* (Philadelphia: Westminster Press, 1960) (hereafter *Institutes*, Book.chapter.section) (1559 edition), 1.6.2, 2.6.4, 2.7.2, 3.2.6. Merwyn Johnson, "Calvin's Handling of the Law," in R.V. Schnunker, *Calviniana: Ideas and Influence of Jean Calvin* (Kirksville, MO.: Sixteenth Century Journal Publishers, 1988), p. 44.

which concerns sin as a general restraint. The law as written in the human heart, and confirmed by social convention, serves to restrain sin through civil and criminal codes. The third use of the law regarded the sanctification of the believer, since it guides the believer to obedience.

In Lutheran circles, the Formula of Concord in Article VI, "Of the Third Use of the Law," confirms the unity of God's law: "Both for penitent and impenitent, for regenerated and unregenerate people the law is and remains one and the same law, namely, the unchangeable will of God."[2] Lutheran dogma includes a discussion of both the law and Gospel:[3] Melancthon, a member of Luther's circle, says "such can come about through the divine word, through a consideration of the punishments on others, or through our own punishment." The needs of humanity, he claims, include "a divine testimony of what is right and of what sin is; so that through the punishment of sin in all men, the unconverted may be converted, and the converted be strengthened in the fear of God."[4] In the last edition of *Loci Communnes* in 1555, Melancthon also affirmed the third use of the law: "The law in this life is necessary that saints may know and have a testimony of the works which please God."[5]

Calvin explains that in its third use the law has two functions. According to his view, Christians are in a relationship with God that depends on Christ's accomplishments and not works of law.

2. Formula of Concord, Article VI, paragraph 6, quoted from *The Book of Concord*, trans. and ed. Theodore G. Tappert (Phil.: Fortress, 1959), p. 481.

3. For a representative survey, see Philip Watson, *Let God be God. An Interpretation of the Theology of Martin Luther* (London: Epworth, 1947), pp. 152ff.; Paul Althaus, *The Theology of Martin Luther* (Phil.: Fortress, 1966), Chap. 19; Eric W. Gritsch and Robert W. Janson, *Lutheranism: The Theological Movement and Its Confessional Writings* (Phil.: Fortress, 1976), pp. 42ff.; Helmut Thielicke, *The Evangelical Faith* (Grand Rapids: Eerdmans, 1982), vol. 3, ch. 11.

4. Melancthon on "Christian Doctrine," *Loci Communes 1555*, trans. and ed. Clyde L. Manschrek (New York: Oxford University Press, 1965), p. 127.

5. Merwyn Johnson, "Calvin's Handling of the of the Law," in R.V. Schnunker, *Calviniana: Ideas and Influence of Jean Calvin* (Kirksville, MO.: Sixteenth Century Journal Publishers, 1988).

The function of the law is to foster in Christians the urge to learn "more thoroughly each day the nature of the Lord's will to which they aspire"[6] A Christian is the servant who is "already prepared with all earnestness of heart to commend himself to his master, must search out and observe his master's ways more carefully in order to conform and accommodate himself to them."[7] Johnson's work on Calvin (1988) says that to Calvin the law is "an indicator of the character and activity of God."[8] The next function of the law (third category) is exhortation, for as Calvin remarks, "the law is to the flesh like a whip to an idle and balky ass, to arouse it to work,"[9] ready to castigate those who continue to sin. He believed in using the law in discouraging sin through warning of consequences and encouraging righteousness with the promise of reward.[10]

Even if the law meets with suitable hosts, it can turn into an occasion that condemns them as sinners.[11] While Calvin and Luther agreed on the three uses of the law, Calvin regarded the third use of the law as a guide for believers as the "principal use."[12] In Calvin's view the civil magistrate had the authority to enforce both tables of the Ten Commandments—that is *pietas* and *aequitas*.[13]

---

6. *Institutes*, 2.7.12, 1.33.

7. *Institutes*, 2.7.12.

8. Merwyn Johnson, "Calvin's Handling of the Law," in R.V., *Calviniana: Ideas and Influence of Jean Calvin* (Kirksville, MO.: Sixteenth Century Journal Publishers, 1988), p. 46.

9. *Institutes* (1536 edition):1.33, 1559:2.7.12.

10. Merwyn Johnson, "Calvin's Handling of the of the Law," in R.V. Schnunker, *Calviniana: Ideas and Influence of Jean Calvin* (Kirksville, MO.: Sixteenth Century Journal Publishers, 1988), p. 47.

11. John Calvin, *Institutes*, 2.7.7; Merwyn Johnson, "Calvin's Handling of the of the Law," in R.V. Schnunker, *Calviniana: Ideas and Influence of Jean Calvin* (Kirksville, MO.: Sixteenth Century Journal Publishers, 1988).

12. John Calvin, *Institutes* 2.7.12; I. John Hesselink, "Law and Gospel Or Gospel and Law?" in R.V. Schnucker, *Calviniana: Ideas and Influence of Jean Calvin* (Kirksville, MO.: Sixteenth Century Journal Publishers, 1988), p. 13.

13. Harro Hopfl, *The Christian Polity of John Calvin* (Cambridge: Cambridge University Press, 1982), p. 172.

CALVIN'S VIEW OF THE SOURCE OF LAW

Luther and Melancthon see God as the source of law. William Maurer, in his excellent commentary on the Augsburg Confession, concludes, "In no way did either Luther or Melancthon see government as the source of property laws, nor could a Christian rest easy in settling all questions about property by referring to specific public laws." In matters of buying and selling, both Luther and Melancthon believed that everyone ought to be able to follow the dictates of conscience.[14] Regarding civic regulation, Luther argues for a decentralized government, allowing local market conditions according to geography and experts authorized to supervise and check transactions.[15]

Calvin on the other hand, sees the politics of civic life as morally derived from both biblical law and natural law. The authority of fathers over their wives and children,[16] monogamy,[17] duty of paternal care for families,[18] breast-feeding,[19] obligation of promises,[20] the need for more than one witness in the case of murder,[21] the

---

14. Wilhelm Maurer, trans. H. George Anderson, *Historical Commentary on the Augsburg Confession* (Phil.: Fortress Press, 1986), p. 156; compare *Luther's Works*, 49:54.

15. Martin Luther, *D. Martin Luthers Werke: Krtische Gesamtausgabe*, (Gutersloh, 1951), vol. 16, 554:27-28; Jaroslav Pelikan and Helmut T. Lehman, eds., *Luthers' Works*, 54 vols. (St. Louis: Concordia Publishing House, 1955), vol. 49, p. 54; vol. 45, pp. 248-51.

16. John Calvin, *Commentaries* (Edinburgh: Calvin Translation Society, 1843-59), 1 Corinthians 7:37; Ephesians 5:31; 1 Timothy 2 and 5:8.

17. John Calvin, *Commentaries* (Edinburgh: Calvin Translation Society, 1843-59), Genesis 26:10; 38:24 (hereafter *Commentaries*, reference).

18. John Calvin, *Commentaries*, 1 Timothy 5:8.

19. John Calvin, *Commentaries*, Genesis 21:8 (primogeniture with some qualifications); John Calvin, *Commentaries*, Genesis 27:11.

20. John Calvin, *Commentaries*, 1 Corinthians 9:1.

21. John Calvin, *Harmony of Moses* (Edinburgh: Calvin Translation Society, 1843-59), III, p. 45.

prohibition of incest,[22] adultery,[23] and slavery,[24] and respect for the old[25] derived from natural law as well as biblical law in Calvin's thinking.[26]

He sees capital punishment as sanctioned by both biblical and natural law, and believed adultery merited capital punishment; however, Calvin does not explain why he believes burning is a valid substitute for biblical stoning:

> The law of God commands adulterers to be stoned. Before this punishment was set down in written law, the adulterous woman was, by the consent of all, committed to the flames. It is established that this was done by a divine instinct, under the direction and teaching of nature, so that the sanctity of marriage might be defended as by a strong guard. How much more vile and how much less excusable is our negligence nowadays, which cherishes adulteries by allowing them to go unpunished. Capital punishment, indeed, is considered too severe for the measure of the offense. Why then do we punish lighter faults with greater rigor? Truly the world was bewitched by Satan when it suffered a law implanted in all by nature to become obsolete.[27]

When Calvin was asked by the Genevan consistory to contribute to the city's codification efforts, to its new laws and edicts, he turned to the Roman *Corpus Juris Civilis* for a model of contract

22. John Calvin, *Commentaries* (Edinburgh: Calvin Translation Society, 1843–59), Genesis 29:27; John Calvin, *Harmony of Moses* (Edinburgh: Calvin Translation Society, 1843–59), III, p. 20.

23. John Calvin, *Commentaries* (Edinburgh: Calvin Translation Society, 1843–59), Genesis 26:10; John Calvin, *Harmony of Moses* (Edinburgh: Calvin Translation Society, 1843–59), III, p. 77.

24. John Calvin, *Harmony of Moses* (Edinburgh: Calvin Translation Society, 1843–59), III, pp. 18, 98.

25. John Calvin, *Commentaries* (Edinburgh: Calvin Translation Society, 1843–59), Genesis 12:15; Ephesians 6:1.

26. Harro Hopfl, *The Christian Polity of John Calvin* (Cambridge: Cambridge University Press, 1982), p. 180.

27. John Calvin, *Commentaries* (Edinburgh: Calvin Translation Society, 1843–59), Genesis 38:24.

law, property law, and judicial procedure.[28] His use of this source signified his belief that natural law was a phenomenon discerned by all nations, irrespective of pagan origins of the lawmakers. (Calvin's drafts are in G. Baum's *Joannis Calvini Opera Quae Supersunt Omnia*.[29]) In the humanist tradition of the day, Calvin expanded his legal studies, as to include other literature, at the suggestion of his friend Bude, who showed Calvin that a study of law and *bonare litterae* (a humanist slogan for good literature) could complement each other.[30] Calvin's theory of law, then, grew with his exposure to legal sources, good literature, and the Bible.

CALVIN'S VIEW OF THE RELATION OF LAW AND THE GOSPEL

The Distinction Between Law and Grace

Readers of Calvin often have interpretive problems regarding his use of the words "law" and "grace." As I. John Hesselink observes: "What is often overlooked by Lutheran scholars who write on this subject and who compare Luther and Calvin is that they are not always talking about the same thing when they use the expression 'law and gospel.' Neither of them uses the expression in a fixed way, so that depending on the situation or context, 'law and gospel' can mean any one of a number of things."[31] In the same vein, Hesselink recommends that readers look at the context before deciding what meaning attaches to the terms: "One cannot make any judgments at all about Calvin's understanding of law and Gospel without

---

28. Harro Hopfl, *The Christian Polity of John Calvin* (Cambridge: Cambridge University Press, 1982), pp. 6-7.

29. G. Baum, E. Cunitz, and E. Reuss, eds. *Joannis Calvini Opera Quae Supersunt Omnia* (Brunswick and Berlin, 1863-1900), 10, I, pp. 125-46.

30. Harro Hopfl, *The Christian Polity of John Calvin* (Cambridge: Cambridge University Press, 1982), p. 7.

31. I. John Hesselink, "Law and Gospel or Gospel and Law?" in R.V. Schnucker, *Calviniana: Ideas and Influence of Jean Calvin* (Kirksville, MO.: Sixteenth Century Journal Publishers, 1988), p. 14.

recognizing the various meanings each of those terms connotes and the various qualifications made within those meanings."[32]

In their commentaries on Galatians, Calvin and Luther display no significant differences on the nature and distinction separating the law from the Gospel.[33] Not only does Calvin make a distinction between the law as a means of salvation, and grace as the means of salvation, but contends there is an antithesis between the two forms.[34] In his commentary on Exodus 19:1, Calvin refers to the law's addition because of trangressions (from Galatians 3:19), meaning one is separated from the promise of grace, and is considered in the light of the law's "peculiar office, power, and end."[35] In this context, Calvin refers to the law as *nuda lex* or "bare law."[36]

The Continuity of Law and Gospel

As scholars, Calvin, Zwingli, Bucer, Melanchthon, and Bullinger agree that God's covenant with Abraham was the same as the New Covenant of Gospels and Epistles.[37] The covenant with Abraham in the Old Testament and believers in the New differ only in outward form. To Calvin, the covenants of the Patriarchs were one

---

32. I. John Hesselink, p. 32.

33. I. John Hesselink, p. 15; John Hesselink, "Luther and Calvin on Law and Gospel in Their Galatians Commentaries," *Reformed Review* 37/2 (Winter 1984); Andrew J. Banstra, "Law and Gospel in Calvin and Paul," in *Exploring the Heritage of John Calvin: Essays in Honor of John Bratt*, ed. David E. Holwerda (Grand Rapids: Baker, 1976).

34. John Calvin, *Institutes*, 2.10.2.

35. John Calvin, *Harmony of the Last Four Books of Moses*, (Grand Rapids: Eerdmans, 1948–50), 1:314.

36. I. John Hesselink, "Law and Gospel or Gospel and Law?" in R.V. Schnucker, *Calviniana: Ideas and Influence of Jean Calvin* (Kirksville, MO.: Sixteenth Century Journal Publishers, 1988), p. 17; *Institutes* 2.7.2.

37. Gottlob Schrenk, *Gottesreich und Bund im alteren Protestantismus* (Darmstadt: Wissenschaftliche Buchgesellschaft, 1967 [reprint 1923]).

with that of the New Testament; they differ only in externals—the *modus administrationis*.³⁸

The *nova docendi forma*, or new mode of instruction, replaced ancient ceremonies, but the *doctrinae substantia*, the substance of doctrine, was unaltered.³⁹ In the former, the doctrine was handed down from the mountain top; in the latter, the Lord's mountain was heaven, the already triumphant church ascended in worship.⁴⁰ Although the doctrine of God is the "same and always agrees with itself" (*et sui perpetuo similem*), the doctrine itself came "out of Zion" with new clothing (*veste*).⁴¹ Law and grace are derived from God's will (*hoc ex Dei ordinatione pendet*).⁴²

Calvin sees Moses as holding two titles (*munera*). On the one hand, he was steward of general doctrine (*generalem doctrinam*), communicating God's message everywhere, law and gospel both (*in universum*); as steward of general doctrine, Moses preached the Gospel (*evangelii praeconem*).⁴³ On the other hand, Moses had a mandate (*mandatum*) to lead the state of the Israelites, since Yahweh had commissioned him to instill obedience to the geopolitical (*propria*) civil and judicial code given at Sinai.⁴⁴

---

38. Calvin, *Institutes*, 2.10.2; 2.11.1; Consider Calvin's argument, more forceful in Latin: "Patrum omnium foedus adeo substantia et re ipsa nihim a nostro differt, ut unum prorsus atque idem sit. Administratio tamen variat." And further, "Eas omne sic esse dico, et ostensurum me profiteor, ut ad modum administrationis potiuos quam ad substantiam pertineant. Hac ratione nihil impedient quominus eaedem maneant veteris ac novi testamenti promissiones, atque idem ipsorum promissionum fundamentum, Christus." Calvin, *Institutes*, 2.10.2; 2.11.1.

39. I. John Hesselink, "Law and Gospel or Gospel and Law?" in R.V. Schnucker, *Calviniana: Ideas and Influence of Jean Calvin* (Kirksville, MO.: Sixteenth Century Journal Publishers, 1988), p. 18; *Commentary*, Isaiah 2:3; contrast Ex. 19:1 with Is. 2:3.

40. Compare Galatians 4:26.

41. *Commentaries*, Isaiah 2:3; I. John Hesselink, "Law and Gospel or Gospel and Law?" in R.V. Schnucker, *Calviniana: Ideas and Influence of Jean Calvin* (Kirksville, MO.: Sixteenth Century Journal Publishers, 1988), p. 18.

42. *Commentaries*, 2 Corinthians 3:6.

43. *Commentaries*, Romans 10:5; *Commentaries*, Exodus 19:1.

44. *Commentaries*, Exodus 19:1; *Commentaries*, Romans 7:2.

THE LEGAL THEORY OF JOHN CALVIN

CALVIN'S VIEW OF THE PROSECUTORIAL FUNCTION OF LAW

Calvin's thinking is a reminder of Augustine's: "If the Spirit of grace is absent, the law is present only to accuse and kill us."[45] Calvin called the Ten Commandments the "bare law," on behalf of which God demands his due (*exigit quod sibi debetur*). But this law does not impart either the ability or desire to perform.[46] The Decalogue is "bare," in the sense of explanation (*cf.* Exodus 21–23), motivation, and the believer's desire and ability to conform.

Calvin distinguishes King David's praises for the law from Paul's condemnation of those who attempt to earn salvation merely by being law abiding. When David praises God's law, as per Psalm 119, he means the law as a whole, which includes the promises of salvation.[47] As Calvin concludes, "If Adam had remained upright (*si integer stetisset Adam*)," (Romans 7:19), "the law would not have brought death upon us."[48] The nature of holy law is both "perpetual and inseparable (*perpetuum et inseparabel*) from its nature. The blessing which it offers to us is excluded by our depravity, so that only the curse remains."[49] He further explains, "God exhibited a remarkable proof of his goodness in promising life to all who kept his law—and this will always remain inviolate (*integrum*)."[50]

Of course, Calvin sees the "bare law" as presenting an impossible challenge to the unregenerate; Jesus Christ alone is able to keep the law. Accordingly, the "wickedness and condemnation of us all are sealed by the testimony of the law. Yet this is not done to cause us to fall down in despair, or completely discouraged, to rush headlong over the brink—provided we duly profit by the

---

45. Augustine quoted in Calvin, *Institutes*, 2.7.7.

46. Calvin, *Commentaries*, 2 Corinthians 3:7.

47. Compare *Commentaries*, Psalm 19:7–8 with *Commentaries*, Acts 7:38 and 2 Corinthians 3:14–17.

48. Calvin, *Institutes*, 1.2.1.

49. Calvin, *Commentaries*, Galatians 3:10.

50. Calvin, *Commentaries*, Ezekiel 20:11.

testimony of the law."[51] In Calvin's opinion, the law's accusatory character should not depress but illumine.

CONCLUSION

Unlike our modern era, Reformation legal theory is monadic—a universal God governs universally through a universal law. Modern Western pluralism views law as a governing entity separate and distinct from religious organizations. "Secular" law stops where organized religion begins. With his Reformer colleagues, Calvin did not view church and society as compartmentalized. Rather, one truth, one church, one society, one government, and one law derived from God through the Bible and nature. Calvin's holistic worldview and the modern pluralistic one are galaxies apart.

---

51. Calvin, *Institutes*, 2.7.8.

THE POLITICAL THEORY OF JOHN CALVIN

The political contribution of John Calvin, although proffered in a time and culture distant from our own, remains of interest and value to our generation. When institutions teeter on the brink of bankruptcy, when nations crunch under unpayable national debt, when streets are battlegrounds, when families are torn by infidelity, perhaps extremity implies a current need to consider the political theory devised by the great Reformer—a biblical expositor of value and reputation.

Calvin advances a doctrine of separation of church and state, not religion and state. Because God is sovereign, Calvin postulates that he should rule both church and state, since both are religious entities predicated on God's authority, even though the two structures are distinct organizations. The state rules the church's environs, maintaining domestic tranquility so that the church can execute a mission to evangelize and make disciples of all citizens. By fostering the maturity of its Christian flock, the church nurtures the state by producing model citizens; thus church and state are mutually inclined.

Over temporal matters, the state was to have jurisdiction; over doctrinal and spiritual matters, the church was to have jurisdiction, though both were to be religious. Theocracy, theonomy, and religiosity were fundamental to Calvin's Reformed society, since he believed that the entire state should be ruled by God, draw its laws from God, and be devoted entirely to him.[1] Calvin's

---

1. John Calvin, *Calvin: Institutes of the Christian Religion*, 2 vols., ed.

political theory includes a distinction of church and state, checks and balances on power, the citizen's submission to the state, and the state's responsibility to God.

CALVIN'S THEORY OF CHURCH AND STATE

Although Calvin's church and state are distinct, their spheres overlap. Ecclesiastically, the church of Geneva was ruled by a representative body, the consistory. Nine pastors, elected by their several congregations, deliberated as men of the cloth; twelve elders, and four syndics (executives), elected democratically by all church members, represented the church. To hold any office, of course, a party had to be a church member in good standing. Voting was a right accorded on the basis of good standing within the church.

According to Calvin, there is a symbiosis of purpose for church and state but there is also a distinction of purpose. The state sets the stage for the church and the church does not obstruct the state.[2] Calvin held that state and church were mutually religious, because the state adjudicated temporal matters under God and the church adjudicated spiritual matters under God, but both opposing evil. Evil—spiritual, social, doctrinal, moral, temporal—was the common enemy that unifies the two divinely instituted bodies. In Calvin's vision, a society that was composed of a Reformed church, and a church comprised of Reformed citizens were a fist that beats back the world and all its evil spiritual, moral, cultural, legal, and political manifestations.[3]

Ecclesiastical and political dimensions of the Genevan community interacted. Ecclesiastically, nominated and elected by the church, the most the consistory could do in church discipline was punish by keeping people from the sacraments. If they were not

---

John T. McNeill and tr. Ford Lewis Battles, *Library of Christian Classics 20-21* (Philadelphia: Westminster Press, 1960) (hereafter *Institutes*, Book.chapter. section) (1559 edition), 2.20.9.

2. E. William Monter, "The Consistory of Geneva," *Enforcing Morality in Early Modern Europe* (London, 1987), pp. 467–484.

3. *Institutes*, 4.20.9.

sufficiently penitent, they were excommunicated, that is, kept from the sacraments (but still allowed to attend services) until they mended their ways.[4] Politically, the impenitent were then remitted to the care of the small council. Three democratically elected bodies ruled the Genevan city-state—the council of 200, the council 60, and the council of 20, or small council. The lower council was popularly elected. The lower council elected the council of 60, and the council of 60 elected the small council, which possessed executive power to punish impenitents. The small council sentenced people to fines, the stocks, imprisonment, banishment, or capital punishment, as a last resort.

Calvin, therefore, envisions church and state as a united force that protects the people. Arnold van Ruler contends that according to Calvin, the state's vision, and *raison de etre*, derives from the church: "The state must have some vision, some insight into the truth, into the essence of things."[5] Van Ruler says that Calvin sees the church's influence upon the state in terms of the First Commandment, the imperative of which encompasses both church and state: "Yahweh is not only critical to the point of grumbling, he also has something intolerant, even imperialistic, about him. He tolerates no other gods beside him. He demands an exclusive obedience of the whole man and his whole life. This has an immediate impact on all aspects of political life."[6] Calvin's God demands an obedience that circumscribes every facet of human existence—sociology, law, government, and politics, as well as religious belief and ritual.

Calvin's view of the relationship uniting church and state is neither Erastian nor "ecclessiocratic," since both schemes deny reciprocity. Erastes advanced the notion that the church is an arm of the state, such as Henry the Eighth's Supremacy Act. In an

---

4. Compare *Institutes*, 4.12.

5. Arnold A. van Ruler, trans. John Bolt, *Calvinist Trinitarianism and Theocentric Politics—Essays Toward a Public Theology* (Lewiston/Queenston/Lampeter: The Edwin Mellen Press, 1989), p. 157.

6. Arnold A. van Ruler, trans. John Bolt, *Calvinist Trinitarianism and Theocentric Politics—Essays Toward a Public Theology* (Lewiston/Queenston/Lampeter: The Edwin Mellen Press, 1989), p. 153.

ecclesiocracy, however, the state is an arm of the church. Church officials, using state institutions, run society—that is, they raise and spend state revenue, settle disputes, provide for the common defense, and regulate the economy and social relations. Calvin envisioned neither. Rather, Calvin envisioned a religious republic, both theocratic and theonomic. In a theocracy, God rules the state and God rules the church. In theonomy, all law derives from God's law. Calvin viewed a Christian state as God's rule by God's law.

Calvin does not, however, insist that all Mosaic judicial law should be enacted and enforced.[7] Instead he denounced totalitarian theonomists of his day who insisted that the "political system of Moses" was mandatory for civil government.[8] If those who represented Geneva's citizenry voted to enact the entire "political system of Moses," Calvin would not have opposed the total enactment, since he saw the "political system of Moses" as an ideal but not mandatory requirement for a Reformed state.

Calvin sees the state as a religious entity and hence as a stabilizing force—this view is recorded in book four: "The External Means or Aids by which God Invites Us into the Society of Christ and Holds Us Therein." In McNeil's edition, however, only thirty-five pages deal with the state—a meager seven percent of the work, the remaining text dedicated to the role of the church.[9]

Calvin sees the necessity for constancy in applying law: "When laws are variable, many are necessarily injured, and no private interest is stable unless the law be without variation; besides, when there is liberty of changing laws, license succeeds in place of justice."[10] Rewards and punishments are "part of a well-ordered administration of a commonwealth." He interprets the term "praise" (Romans 13:1–7) according to its Semitic biblical

7. *Institutes*, 4.20.14, n. 36.

8. *Institutes*, 4.20.14.

9. W. Fred Graham, "Calvin and the Political Order: An Analysis of the Three Explanatory Studies," in R.V. Schnucker, ed., *Calviana: Ideas and Influence of Jean Calvin* (Kirksville, MO.: Sixteenth Century Journal Publishers, 1988), p. 55.

10. John Calvin, "Commentaries on Daniel," *On God and Political Duty* (Indianapolis: Bobbs-Merrill, 1956), p. 92.

origins, and its meaning is various.[11] Calvin sees the term "praise" as general benefit, including protection and prosperity.

Graham's thesis on Calvin's treatment of the state is inimical—"Calvin's political theory is weak and unhelpful, his practice as an influencer of the magistrates of Geneva overly harsh, lacking in the generally pragmatic approach Calvin took toward matters that were not at the heart of the gospel."[12] Graham continues:

> The Christian gospel, which proclaims the love of God inextricably bound up with Jesus Christ, whose compassion for humankind took him even to the Cross, if this good news will not have a beneficial effect on men in society when once it grips a man of Calvin's stature—then it is of dubious value ... But if the gospel at times became a club, an excuse for foolishness and insensitivity, for torture, even death. What went wrong?. . . Contemporaries of lesser acumen than Calvin in neighboring cities were perplexed by this rigor, that, had St. Paul applied it, would have excommunicated every person in Corinth.[13]

In sum, Calvin views both church and state as unified by the overarching purpose of arresting evil but separated by a porous membrane—a membrane dividing their respective functions into spheres, one sphere focusing on the spiritual, the other on the temporal. To Calvin, church and state were to be two hands washing each other under God.

---

11. John Calvin, "Commentaries on the Epistle to the Romans, Chapter XIII:3," *On God and Political Duty* (Indianapolis: Bobbs-Merrill, 1956), p. 86.

12. W. Fred Graham, "Calvin and the Political Order: An Analysis of the Three Explanatory Studies," in R.V. Schnucker, ed., *Calviana: Ideas and Influence of Jean Calvin* (Kirksville, MO.: Sixteenth Century Journal Publishers, 1988), p. 55.

13. W. Fred Graham, "Constructive Revolutionary," R.V. Schnucker, ed., *Calviana: Ideas and Influence of Jean Calvin* (Kirksville, MO.: Sixteenth Century Journal Publishers, 1988), pp. 174–76.

CALVIN'S THEORY OF CHECKS AND BALANCES ON POLITICAL POWER

Calvin sees tyranny as the demon that stalks the state, seeking to possess it. Tyranny is threatened whenever power is in the hands of the few. To him, power unchecked is power unjustified, since he believes that too often power, especially absolute power, has corrupted those hold it. He sees absolute power as so corrupting that those in power cannot call themselves "ministers of God" (Romans 13:1–7). Indeed the powerful sank to a level where there was "no trace of that minister of God, who had been appointed to praise the good, and to punish the evil." According to Calvin, state officers (Romans 13:1–7) were good, though evil might eclipse the good, to such a degree one could see them no longer as a moral force.[14]

Calvin sees the danger of entrusting power to one or a few; accordingly he argues for a "system compounded of aristocracy and democracy."[15] McNeil believes that Calvin's reference to the "rule of principal persons" does not refer to blood aristocracy but rather to those chosen by their fellows.[16] To Calvin, the presence of any hereditary ruling caste is an infringement of liberty.[17] States are better ruled by elected officials, ruling under law, than royalty:

> If we argue about human governments we can say that to be in a free state is much better than to be under a prince. It is much more endurable to have rulers who are chosen and elected . . . and who acknowledge themselves subject to the laws, than to have a prince who gives utterance without reason.[18]

---

14. *Institutes*, 4.20.25.

15. *Institutes*, 4.20.7.

16. John T. McNeill, "Calvin and Civil Government," in Donald McKim, ed., *Readings in Calvin's Theology* (Grand Rapids: Baker, 1984), p. 273.

17. John T. McNeill, "Calvin and Civil Government," p. 273.

18. Jean Calvin, *Ioannis Calvini Opera quae supersunt omnia. Ad fidem.* eds. Guilielmus Baum, Eduardus Cunitz, and Eduardus Reuss (Brunsvigae: Appelhans & Pfenningstorff, 1890), vol. 43, p. 374.

Calvin sees as the highest good a state that is governed by elected representatives. In other words, the original Hebrew state is categorized as a theocractic theonomic republic: "I readily acknowledge that no kind of government is more happy than this, where liberty is regulated with becoming moderation and properly established on a durable foundation (*ad diuturnitatem*)."[19] In February 1560, on the eve of an election, Calvin pleaded with the General Assembly "to choose [their magistrates] with a pure conscience, without regard to anything but the honor and glory of God, for the safety and defense of the republic."[20] Because he believed that the republic was the highest form of government, the highest form of loyalty to country was that given to a Christian republic.

In Calvin's thinking, theocracy and democracy are "easily and naturally associated."[21] The civil government has the God-given burden of maintaining peace and tranquility, so that the church can flourish:

> Yet civil government has as its appointed end, so long as we live among men, to cherish and protect the outward worship of God, to defend sound doctrine of piety and the position of the church, to adjust our life to the society of men, to form our social behavior to civil righteousness, to reconcile us with one another, and to promote general peace of tranquility . . .[22]

Calvin, however, includes within the state's ambit the defense of "sound doctrine," a doctrine that may strike us as strange today but was the norm in Calvin's time:

> Let no man be disturbed that I now commit to civil government the duty of rightly establishing religion, which I seem above to have put outside of human decision. For, when I approve of a civil administration that aims

---

19. *Institutes*, 4.20.8.

20. John T. McNeill, "Calvin and Civil Government," in Donald McKim, ed., *Readings in Calvin's Theology* (Grand Rapids: Baker, 1984), p. 274.

21. John T. McNeill, "Calvin and Civil Government," p. 274.

22. *Institutes*, 4.20.3.

to prevent the true religion which is contained in God's law from being openly and with public sacrilege violated and defiled with impunity, I do not here, any more than before, allow men to make laws according to their own decision concerning religion and the worship of God.[23]

Neither does he advocate that governments necessarily enact all the Old Testament judicial laws.[24] Indeed, he denounces the radical theonomists of his day who insisted that the "political system of Moses" was mandatory for civil government.[25] Mosaic judicial law was the ideal but not the immediate requirement in Calvin's thinking.

For Calvin, the highest form of political development is representative democracy, modeled on the biblical example:

> In this consists the best condition of the people, when they can choose, by common consent, their own shepherds; for when any one by force usurps the supreme power, it is tyranny, and when men become kings by hereditary right, it seems not consistent with liberty.[26]

In his lectures on Amos 7, Calvin rebukes civil authorities in England and Germany,[27] saying that Henry VIII appointing himself the head of the church was a "blasphemy." Neither should princes in Germany "become chief judges as in doctrine as in all spiritual government," but rather, they should support the Church, using their temporal power to "render free the worship of God."[28] When a city-state comes under the influence of God's Word, then that body is held to a higher function:

---

23. *Institutes*, 4.20.3.
24. *Institutes*, 4.20.26, n. 36.
25. *Institutes*, 4.20.26.
26. John Calvin, *Commentaries on the Twelve Minor Prophets III* (Grand Rapids: Eerdmans, 1948), pp. 306–310 (Micah 5:5).
27. John Calvin, *Commentaries on the Twelve Minor Prophets II* (Grand Rapids: Eerdmans, 1950), p. 349 (Amos 7:10–13).
28. John Calvin, *Commentaries on the Twelve Minor Prophets II* (Grand Rapids: Eerdmans, 1950), pp. 349–50 (Amos 7:10–13).

> When a city becomes renowned for having received the Word of God, the world will reckon that the city ought to be, as a result, so much better governed, that such order will there prevail as to accord right and justice to one and all.[29]

The Reformation did not originate the political theories that dominated the seventeenth and eighteenth centuries, but it did accelerate and intensify the growth of theories that existed already.[30] Early in the Reformation, the monarchs of Spain, France, Scotland, the Netherlands, and to some extent England, were polemic Catholics ready to stamp out Protestantism. The Reformation began at the local level, among estates, cities, provinces, and the nobility, as it expanded enveloping those who opposed all absolutist practices. Absolutism is a presence in the scholarship of the Renaissance, as well as featuring in Reformation writings.[31] The Reformation had to contend with proponents of absolutism, who rejected its pluralism,[32] preferring instead to believe in one God, one king, one creed and one law.[33]

A variety of theorists argue for the sovereignty of the people in contradistinction to the sovereignty of a monarch—Marsilius of Padua, Occam, Ptolemaeus of Lucca, Bartolus, Gerson, d'Ailly, and Cusanus.[34] Each of these teaches that under natural law people's sovereignty is protected by a political contract that binds both ruler and subjects.[35] Italian humanists see the self-governing city-state as a breeding ground for anti-monarchist tendencies. Machiavelli, for instance, argued, "Where there are many states, there

---

29. Alastair Duke, trans. and ed., "Calvin the Preacher—Extracts from Calvin's Sermons on Micah" in *Calvinism in Europe 1540–1610—A Collection of Documents* (Manchester: Manchester University Press, 1992).

30. Hans Baron, "Calvinist Republicanism and its Historical Roots," *Church History* 8 (1939), p. 32.

31. Hans Baron, p. 33.

32. Hans Baron, p. 34.

33. Hans Baron, p. 32.

34. Hans Baron, p. 32.

35. Hans Baron, p. 32.

arise many efficient men; where the states are few, the efficient men are rare."³⁶ The Italian humanists wanted to restore the Republica Romana, a state where people were free. Martin Bucer, a contemporary of the Italian Machiavelli, desired a restoration of the early Israelite confederacy before the Kingdom of Saul (*cf.* 1 Sam. 8:15ff.), the state of a free people.³⁷ The reformation at Strassbourg mirrored the paradigm shift of the Italian city-states, Nuremberg and Strassbourg (particularly Strassbourg) being economically self-sufficient as well as self-governing German city-states.³⁸

According to Martin Bucer, the existence of *magistratus inferiores*, that is of self-governing city-state authorities, is a product of an historical political development that is directed by God. Any overlord who tries to limit the authority of minor powers is acting against the will of God. All minor authorities must protect and beautify the Sparta that had been entrusted to them by God, against encroachments of a higher power that threatens the true religion.³⁹

In his *Lectures on the Book of Judges*, Bucer states that "wherever absolute power is given to a prince, there the glory and the dominion of God is injured. The absolute power, which is God's alone, would be given to a man liable to sin."⁴⁰ Bucer, a contemporary of Machiavelli, recognizes the benefits of husbanding one's resources in times of need, reminding his readers that the Roman

---

36. Hans Baron, "Calvinist Republicanism and its Historical Roots," *Church History* 8 (1939), pp. 33-34; Machiavelli, *Arte della Guerra, in Opere* (Italia, 1813), vol. 4, p. 271.

37. Hans Baron, "Calvinist Republicanism and its Historical Roots," *Church History* 8 (1939), pp. 36-37.

38. Hans Baron, p. 35.

39. Hans Baron, p. 36.

40. Hans Baron, "Calvinist Republicanism and its Historical Roots," *Church History* 8 (1939): 30-42; Martin Bucer, *In Librum Judicum Enarrationes* (Geneva, 1554), p. 448; *cf.* Martin Bucer, *Acta colloquij in comitjs Imerij Ratisponae habiti, hoc est articuli de religione conciliati, & non conciliati omnes, ut ab Imperatore Ordinibus Imperij ad iudicandum, & deliberandum propositi sunt* (Argentorati [Per Vuendelinum Ribeliu], 1542).

republic allowed for dictatorial emergency powers when that was necessary.[41] Calvin agrees with Bucer.

Because the absolute power of princes diminishes the sovereignty of God, grounds for limiting the princes are religious ones.[42] If the power over others is hereditary, then the prince's capacity to judge according to God's judgment is limited[43]:

> There ought to be room for divine selection of those whom God will place at the helm of the state, and whom He benefits with the spirit of His wisdom. Elective monarchy, and not a hereditary kingdom, is the constitution favored by religion. This, stated Bucer, would be the ideal order of a state: either one or a few men would have the power; but these men ought to be designated by God. They would govern on the basis of a legal order. Absolute power would not be conferred on any ruler.[44]

Israel's offer of a throne to Gideon, who had rescued the nation, was justified, but conferring royal power by hereditary right to Gideon's family was *vitiosum et impium*—impious.[45] Calvin later argues for the *magistratus populares*, the ephors of the people, elected by the people for the people.[46] Confirming Bucer's views, Calvin's own works are published after Bucer's *Lectures on the Book of Judges* in 1554.[47]

Calvin urges moderation on a sovereign, remarking as he does so "that no virtue is so rare in kings as moderation, and yet none is more necessary; for the more they have in the power, the more it becomes them to be cautious lest they indulge their lusts, while they think it lawful to desire whatever pleases them."[48]

41. Martin Bucer, *In Librum Judicum Enarrationes* (Geneva, 1554), p. 473.
42. Hans Baron, "Calvinist Republicanism and its Historical Roots," *Church History* 8 (1939):37.
43. Hans Baron, pp. 37–38.
44. Hans Baron, p. 38.
45. Hans Baron, pp. 30–42.
46. Hans Baron, p. 38.
47. Hans Baron, p. 39.
48. John Calvin, "Commentaries on Daniel," *On God and Political Duty*,

Moreover, he warns them not to be ruled by their subjects. "Thus princes also who are not free agents through being under the tyranny of others, if they permit themselves to be overcome contrary to their conscience, lay aside all their authority and are drawn aside in all directions by the will of their subjects."[49] In the *Harmony of the Last Four Books of Moses*, Calvin voices his approval of classical republican traditions: "In as much as God had given them the use of the franchise, the best way to preserve their liberty for ever was by maintaining a condition of rough equality, lest a few persons of immense wealth should oppress the general body. Since, therefore, the rich, if they had been permitted constantly to increase their wealth, would have tyrannized over the rest, God put a restraint on immoderate power by means of this law."[50] Calvin does not identify an ideal way to govern, nor does he denounce the monarch, recognizing that good government was a prerogative of kings (as he exhorted Francis I). However, Calvin's frequent disparagement of ungodly kings, as per his 1554 sermons on Job, Deuteronomy in 1554–55, and lectures on Daniel in 1561, comprise convincing denunciations of "kings" in general.[51] We cannot regard him as a monarchist, for there is evidence aplenty that he was not.

Men's vices and inadequacies make it safer and better that the many (*plures*) hold sway (*gubernacula*). In this way may rulers help each other, teach and admonish one another, and if one asserts himself unfairly, they may act in concert to censure, repressing his willfulness (*libidinem*).[52] Calvin differs from Aquinas, who in the second chapter of *The Governance of Princes* argues for a

(Indianapolis: Bobbs-Merrill, 1956), p. 94.

49. John Calvin, "Commentaries on Daniel," *On God and Political Duty*, (Indianapolis: Bobbs-Merrill, 1956), pp. 100–1.

50. John Calvin, *Harmony of Moses*, (Edinburgh: Calvin Translation Society, 1843–59), vol. 3, p. 154.

51. John T. McNeill, "Calvin and Civil Government," in Donald McKim, ed., *Readings in Calvin's Theology* (Grand Rapids: Baker, 1984), p. 270.

52. *Institutes*, 4.20.8.

monarchy for the sake of national unity, and to remove the danger of the many tyrannizing the few.[53]

Calvin views 2 Thessalonians 3:15 as evidence of the virtue of "fraternal correction." In his thinking, mutual admonition provides checks and balances against arrogance, believing in it so thoroughly he has "fraternal correction" incorporated into the constitution of the church at Geneva. So saying, in 1557 Calvin influenced the Little Council, the chief deliberative body for civil government, to admonish the recalcitrant in secret "fraternal charity" sessions that met quarterly.[54]

From Micah 5:5, Calvin interprets r ʻh to mean rulers: "For the condition of the people most to be desired is that in which they create their shepherds by general vote (*communibus suffragiis*). When anyone usurps the supreme power by force, that is tyranny. In addition, where men are born to kingship, this does not accord with liberty. Hence, the prophet says: we shall set up princes for ourselves; that is, the Lord will not only give the church freedom to breathe, but also institute a definite and well-ordered government, and establish this upon the common suffrages of all."[55]

Calvin might well agree with Knox's statement: "To bridle the fury and rage of princes in free kingdoms and realms . . . it pertains to the nobility, sworn and born to be councilors of the same, and also to the barons and people, whose votes and consent are to be required in all great and weighty matters of the commonwealth."[56] In 1 Samuel 8, Samuel warns that an absolute monarch with command of judicial, legislative, and executive powers would oppress the people. In his first proposition, Samuel contends, "And this will be the manner (*mšpt*) of the king that shall reign over you . . ."

---

53. John T. McNeill, "Calvin and Civil Government," in Donald McKim, ed., *Readings in Calvin's Theology* (Grand Rapids: Baker, 1984), p. 272.

54. John T. McNeill, "Calvin and Civil Government," p. 272.

55. Jean Calvin, *Ioannis Calvini Opera quae supersunt omnia. Ad fidem.* eds. Guilielmus Baum, Eduardus Cunitz, and Eduardus Reuss, (Brunsvigae: Appelhans & Pfenningstorff, 1890), vol. 43, p. 374.

56. John T. McNeill, "Calvin and Civil Government," in Donald McKim, ed., *Readings in Calvin's Theology* (Grand Rapids: Baker, 1984), p. 273.

(8:11; Calvin gives the French *"puissance"* for *mšpt*, implying that he sees the word in terms of a legal right.)[57]

CALVIN'S THEORY OF THE CITIZEN'S RELATION TO GOVERNMENT

Regardless of the particular form of government, in Calvin's view all subjects of that state are responsible for their own obedience:

---

57. W. Fred Graham, "Calvin and the Political Order: An Analysis of the Three Explanatory Studies," in R.V. Schnucker, ed., *Calviana: Ideas and Influence of Jean Calvin* (Kirksville, MO.: Sixteenth Century Journal Publishers, 1988), p. 53; Keith W. Whitelam, *The Just King: Monarchical Judicial Authority in Ancient Israel* (Sheffield: JSOT Press, 1970). Whitelam traces the legal and political ideal through Ancient Near Eastern cultures and concludes that "it was the king's primary duty to guarantee the true administration of justice throughout the land. By so doing, this governed not only right social relationships, as expressed in the king's concern for the underprivileged, but also guaranteed prosperity and fertility for the nation as a whole." Whitelam derives his conclusion from the Mesopotamian sources of Ur-Nammu, Lipit-Ishtar, Eshnunna, the Syro-Palestinian sources of Alalakh, Ras Shamra, and the Yehimilk inscription, the Egyptian sources of the Kuban Stele of Rameses II, the tale of Merneptah, the Inscriptions of Mentuhotep, and most importantly those of the Babylonian king Hammurabi.

Sources of law in pre-monarchical Israel include family law (ba tyb; Gen. 31; 38; cf. 2 Kgs. 14:6; Deut 24:16; Jer. 31:29-30; Ez. 14:12-20; 18:10-20), clan law, and sacral law. Whitelam concludes the following three-tiered system. Adjudication occurred first with the paterfamilias in the patriarchal family. Aggrieved parties in family-level adjudication could appeal to the clan in rural settings or to the town in urban settings. Both clans and towns were ruled by regional councils of elders. Further, aggrieved parties could appeal from clan and town level adjudication to the local Levitical priests.

On the one hand, Whitelam observes limitations on the authority of the paterfamilias deriving from Numbers 5:11-31, Deuteronomy 21:18-21, and Deuteronomy 22:13-21. In the latter passage, the paterfamilias no longer has the authority to impose the death penalty (unlike Jacob's authority to impose capital punishment on Judah in Genesis 38). On the other hand, Whitelam underscores the apparent breakdown of family solidarity and prophetic rebuke in Isaiah 1:17, Jeremiah 7:6 and 22:13-21.

Extrapolating from the priest's judicial function is the case of undetected adultery (Num. 5:11-31) and the Urim and Thumim, Whitelam concludes that priests were a higher tier of judicial review.

> Subjects should be led not by fear alone of princes and rulers to remain in subjection under them (as they commonly yield to an armed enemy who sees that vengeance is promptly taken if they resist), but because they are showing obedience to God himself when they give it to them; since the rulers' power is from God.[58]

Since a ruler's authority is from God, his citizens are obliged to obey the ruler, no matter what the ruler's character might be:

> I am not discussing the men themselves ... but I say that the order itself is worthy of such honor and reverence and that those who are rulers are esteemed among us, and receive reverence out of respect for their lordship.[59]

> We are not only subject to the authority of princes who perform their office toward us uprightly and faithfully as they ought, but also to the authority of all who, by whatever means, have got control of affairs, even though they perform not a whit of the princes' office.[60]

Calvin views the higher authorities as having been "placed there by the Lord's hand," and rebellion against these authorities as rebellion against God himself—"he who attempts to invert the order of God, and thus to resist God himself, despises his power; since to despise the providence of him who is the founder of civil power, is to carry on without him." The purpose of these acts of providence is the "preservation of legitimate order."[61]

Magistrates have a duty to resist tyranny, but in general, unjust rulers were to be viewed as a judgment from God:

> They who rule unjustly and incompetently have been raised up by him to punish the wickedness of the people; that all equally have been endowed with that holy majesty with which he has invested lawful power.... In a very wicked man utterly unworthy of all honor, provided he

---

58. *Institutes*, 4.20.22.
59. *Institutes*, 4.20.22.
60. *Institutes*, 4.20.25.

61. John Calvin, "Commentaries on the Epistle to the Romans, Chapter XIII:2," *On God and Political Duty*, (Indianapolis: Bobbs-Merrill, 1956), p. 84.

> has the public power in his hands, that noble and divine power resides which the Lord has by his Word given to the ministers of justice and judgment. Accordingly, he should be held in the same reverence and esteem by his subjects, in so far as public obedience is concerned, in which they would hold the best of kings if he were given to them.[62]
>
> Therefore, if we are cruelly tormented by a savage prince, if we are greedily despoiled by one who is avaricious or wanton, if we are neglected by a slothful one, if finally we are vexed for piety's sake by one who is impious and sacrilegious, let us first be mindful of our own misdeeds, which without doubt are chastised by such whips of the Lord. By this, humility will restrain our impatience. Let us then also call this thought to mind, that it is not for us to remedy such evils; that only this remains, to implore the Lord's help, in whose hand are the hearts of kings, and the changing of kingdoms.[63]

Drawing on Romans 13:3, Calvin exhorts his readers to accept that a wicked prince is the result of divine judgment visited upon the governed as punishment for their sins—"For since the wicked prince is the Lord's scourge to punish the sins of the people, let us remember that it happens through our fault that this excellent blessing of God is turned into a curse."[64] He continues in the same vein:

> There are indeed always some tumultuous spirits who believe that the kingdom of Christ cannot be sufficiently elevated unless all earthly powers be abolished, and that they cannot enjoy liberty given by him except they shake off every yoke of human subjection. This error, however, possessed the minds of the Jews above all others; for it seemed to them disgraceful that the offspring of Abraham, whose kingdom flourished before the Redeemer's

---

62. *Institutes*, 4.20.25.

63. *Institutes*, 4.20.26.

64. John Calvin, "Commentaries on the Epistle to the Romans, Chapter XIII:1," *On God and Political Duty*, (Indianapolis: Bobbs-Merrill, 1956), p. 85.

coming, should now, after his appearance continue in submission to another power.[65]

Thomism requires submission to secular authorities. Aquinas argues that "our flesh was still in subjection; we can but await a freedom both of spirit and body, 'when Christ shall have delivered all the kingdoms to God the Father, when he shall have brought to naught all principality and power.' "[66] Similarly, in the *Institutes*, Calvin does not advance an argument for revolution,[67] since to him a ruler is appointed by the providence of God, whether good or evil. If benevolent, the ruler is a blessing; if not, the ruler is a curse. Nebuchadnezzar was still God's servant, even though he served only as an instrument of divine chastisement, and Calvin calls him a "pestilent and cruel tyrant."[68] When ruled by wicked persons, believers must not resist, but instead consider their sins, repent, and implore divine help. Providence will lay proud tyrants low; and moreover, God will raise up leaders who are his appointed instruments.[69]

In a commentary on Romans, written in 1539, Calvin forbids any "private man" from seizing government from a ruler who is appointed by God[70] as the "higher" power (Romans 13:1-7); but the "highest" power, God, people must obey above any other (Acts 5:29).[71] Calvin's last edition of the *Institutes* draws on biblical support for the contention that citizens' highest allegiance is to God, if God and government conflict (Daniel 6:22-23). Here, in Daniel 6, the king has abrogated (*abrogaverit*) his right to reign by raising his hand against God. Hosea 5:11 reminds us that people who

---

65. John Calvin, "Commentaries on the Epistle to the Romans, Chapter XIII:1," *On God and Political Duty*, (Indianapolis: Bobbs-Merrill, 1956), p. 83.

66. Thomas Gilbey, *The Political Thought of Thomas Aquinas* (Chicago: University of Chicago, 1958), p. 157.

67. John T. McNeill, "Calvin and Civil Government," in Donald McKim, ed., *Readings in Calvin's Theology* (Grand Rapids: Baker, 1984), p. 268.

68. John T. McNeill, "Calvin and Civil Government," p. 268.

69. John T. McNeill, "Calvin and Civil Government," p. 268.

70. John T. McNeill, "Calvin and Civil Government," p. 268.

71. John T. McNeill, "Calvin and Civil Government," p. 269.

submit to the religious decrees of an idolatrous king have merited God's condemnation.

In his discussion of rebellion, Calvin argues that it is both the duty and responsibility of popular magistrates to protect people from the license of kings (*populares magistratus ad moderadnam regum libidinem*). He applauds the ephors of Sparta, the Roman tribunes, and the demarchs of Athens for their observance of this principle. To Calvin, the Three Estates (lower magistrates) of the modern kingdoms have not only the right but the obligation to oppose an idolatrous king's violence and cruelty. For a king to "betray the liberty of the people" is a "nefarious perfidy."[72] Calvin believed that lower magistrates, when confronted with a choice between obeying God or obeying a higher magistrate, should obey God.

Calvin believed the lower magistrates of England, Scotland, Sweden, Denmark, Norway, Poland, Bohemia, Hungary, Spain, the diets of the Swiss Confederation, and the imperial diets of Germany should assume the role of the Spartan ephors, thus limiting the tyranny of idolatrous kings.[73] Although citizens must submit to government, Calvin argues these magistrates should not "wink at kings who violently fall upon and assault the lowly common folk."[74] Author John McNeil remarks that in "all these European organs of quasi-representative government he saw at least the possibility of some guarantee of liberty and security for the people."[75] This rationale for political resistance inspired John Knox, John Penot, Christopher Goodman, Francis Hotman, and Samuel Rutherford in their moves against the state and its spiritual profligacy.

> Here is the substance of Calvin's thinking about submitting to and resisting oppressive regimes:
>
> Though we are under Turks, under tyrants, and under the deadly enemies of the gospel, yet is it commanded us

---

72. *Institutes*, 4.20.31; John T. McNeill, "Calvin and Civil Government," in Donald McKim, ed., *Readings in Calvin's Theology* (Grand Rapids: Baker, 1984), p. 270.

73. John T. McNeill, "Calvin and Civil Government," pp. 269-70.

74. *Institutes*, 4.20.31.

75. John T. McNeill, "Calvin and Civil Government," p. 270.

to submit ourselves unto them. Why so? Even because it pleases God.[76]

There are always some restless spirits who believe that the kingdom of Christ is properly exalted only when all earthly powers are abolished, and that they can enjoy the liberty which he had given them only if they have shaken off every yoke of human slavery.[77]

For although the administration of earthly or civil sovereignty is disorderly and corrupt, yet the Lord wishes submission to it to remain unaffected. But when the spiritual rule degenerates the consciences of the godly are released from obedience to an unjust domination, especially if impious and profane enemies of holiness make a false pretense to the title of the priesthood to destroy the doctrine of salvation, and arrogate to themselves a lordship by which God Himself is reduced to order.[78]

Therefore every office of dignity, which has been instituted for the preservation of the civil order, ought to be respected scrupulously, and held in honor. For whoever rises in rebellion against the magistrate, and those endowed with authority or official standing, is striving after anarchy. But a passion of that sort tends to the disruption of order, yes, and what is more, deals a shattering blow to humanity itself.[79]

Christians are free to protest, however "they may not boil over in anger, and match injury with injury . . . but strive to overcome evil with goodness. This does not prevent them from complaining of the injuries done to them, or from convicting the ungodly of their guilt, by summoning them before the judgment of God, provided

---

76. John Calvin, *Commentaries on the Book of Titus* (Grand Rapids: Baker, 1981), vol. 21, pp. 323–24 (Titus 3:1).

77. John Calvin, *Commentaries on the Book of Romans* (Grand Rapids: Baker, 1981), vol. 19, pp. 477–79 (Romans 13:1).

78. John Calvin, *Commentaries on the Book of Acts* (Grand Rapids: Baker, 1981), vol. 19, pp. 317–19 (Acts 23:5).

79. John Calvin, *Commentaries on the Book of Acts* (Grand Rapids: Baker, 1981), vol. 19, pp. 315–16 (Acts 23:5).

that they do so with a calm mind and without ill-will or hatred," for as Calvin concludes, "the spirit of meekness rules in us."[80]

CALVIN'S THEORY OF THE RELATION OF GOVERNMENT TO GOD

Calvin opposes the idea of forwarding Christianity by the sword:

> Although godly kings defend Christ's kingdom by the sword, it is done differently from the way in which worldly kingdoms are defended. For Christ's kingdom, which is spiritual, must be founded on the teaching and power of the Spirit. In the same way is its building effected; for neither the laws and edicts of men nor their punishments reach into consciences, yet this does not prevent princes from incidentally defending Christ's kingdom, partly by establishing external discipline and partly by lending their protection to the Church against the ungodly. But the depravity of the world causes the kingdom of Christ to be established more by the blood of martyrs than by the aid of arms.[81]

Calvin's view is that magistrates too are subject to God's glory—"We know how earthly empires are constituted by God, only on the condition that he deprives himself of nothing, but shines forth alone, and all magistrates must be set in regular order, and every authority in existence must be subject to his glory."[82]

Government, endowed by God with the power of coercion (Romans 13:1–7), is responsible to God. The phrase "minister of God" means, in Calvin's exegesis, one responsible, accountable, and answering to God.[83] Therefore, political authorities, regard-

---

80. John Calvin, *Commentaries on the Book of Acts* (Grand Rapids: Baker, 1981), vol. 19, pp. 317–19 (Acts 23:3).

81. John Calvin, *Commentaries on the Book of John* (Grand Rapids: Baker Book House, 1981), vol. 18, pp. 209–11 (John 18:36).

82. John Calvin, "Commentaries on Daniel," *On God and Political Duty*, (Indianapolis: Bobbs-Merrill, 1956), p. 101.

83. John Calvin, *Commentaries on the Book of Romans* (Grand Rapids: Baker, 1981), vol. 19, pp. 477ff. (Romans 13:1–7).

less of how they are installed, must obey God. Their function is to be regulated by God, who communicates his manifold will to them by his word.[84]

CONCLUSION

Calvin, a man of his day, approaches the matters of law, public policy, and political science from presuppositions different from those shaping modern statecraft. Calvin does not distinguish religion from life, including political life, for to Calvin, religion is all of life and all life is religion. Therefore, all life, law, and politics are not separate from religion but are religion. Further, Calvin did not approach politics from the perspective of Kantian dualism—the "noumenal" and "phenomenal" realms were both subject to God's law, a holy monism. To Calvin, all law, whether moral, civil, or religious, derives from God and God pervades all things. Calvin's view of the institutions of church and state, checks and balances on power, the citizen's relation to government, and government's relation to God are derivations from his religion.

The modern secularist will find Calvin's political views distant, almost otherworldly. Calvin did not labor under the sacred/secular dualism that characterizes current prevailing cultural values. Although Calvin's premises may be considered outmoded in our day, his hatred of tyranny, love of limited government, and passion for justice are values we cannot ignore.

---

84. John Calvin, *Commentaries on the Book of Romans* (Grand Rapids: Baker, 1981), vol. 19, pp. 477ff. (Romans 13:1–7).

THE ROLE OF THE CONSISTORY AT GENEVA

The Republic of Geneva's consistory governed between 18,000 and 19,000 people (1559–69), only half of whom were old enough to take communion. Excommunication was the most common form of social regulation, though hardly permanent. In only a few instances were people excommunicated for good. One man who sold his child into slavery, for example, was permanently excommunicated. Excommunication meant exclusion from holy communion, which was offered four times per year; this exclusion resulted in a social stigma. Some were excommunicated several times per year. By 1569, one in twenty-five individuals had been excommunicated, at some stage, the number of offenders serving to erode the sense of stigma. The society itself could sustain only so much in the way of discipline.[1]

The Consistory included twelve lay elders, chosen annually by the city's magistrates. One of the four syndics, who governed the city with their executive power, presided over the Consistory, which met every Thursday. The Consistory was composed also of between nine and nineteen pastors who labored in the city.[2]

The Consistory was Geneva's public policy-making "think tank." The most the Consistory could do in executive action was excommunicate, forbid the Lord's Supper. The Consistory set

---

1. E. William Monter, "The Consistory of Geneva," *Enforcing Morality in Early Modern Europe* (London, 1987), pp. 467–84.

2. E. William Monter, "The Consistory of Geneva," pp. 467–84.

public policy; the various elected councils of Geneva enacted and executed law consistent with its policies. (Because the Consistory controlled policy, parties would often appeal to the Consistory, not the councils.)

ECONOMIC STRICTURES

In his discussion of capitalism and religion, Martin Butzer foreshadows the views of many Puritans.[3] Lewis Mumford, as cited by Graham, argues that one reason why the Greek city-states failed was no "moralized trade."[4] Regarding usury, for instance, in Calvin's Ecclesiastical Ordinances of May 17, 1547, he says: "Let no one lend at usury or for profit higher than five percent, under penalty of confiscation of the principal, and of being assessed an arbitrary fine according to the requirements of the case."[5] Only Sunday, the day of resurrection, was a day of rest by Genevan law. Because some were celebrating festivals on the Sabbath, city ordinances ordered that each ought to work as has already been proclaimed without celebrating festivals except on Sunday, and this should be commanded district by district under penalty.[6]

Labor unions were forbidden: "Item: that no laborer nor other workers may plot together in order to divert the course of the above proclamations and ordinances, under penalty of being chastised according to the exigency of the case."[7] R. H. Tawney claims that the Venerable Company of Pastors in the Consistory freed the "cannon balls of Christian Socialism." Actually, none of

---

3. Georg Klingenburg, *Das Verhaltnis Calvins zu Butzer auf Grund der wirtschaftsethischen Bedeutung beider Reformatoren* (Bonn, 1912).

4. W. Fred Graham, *The Constructive Revolutionary—John Calvin and His Socio-Economic Impact* (Atlanta: John Knox Press, 1971), p. 116.

5. W. Fred Graham, *The Constructive Revolutionary—John Calvin and His Socio-Economic Impact*, p. 119.

6. W. Fred Graham, *The Constructive Revolutionary—John Calvin and His Socio-Economic Impact*, p. 128.

7. W. Fred Graham, *The Constructive Revolutionary—John Calvin and His Socio-Economic Impact*, p. 142.

the Consistory's policies were socialist. Unlike the Hutterites, who applied the principle of love to the common ownership of property, under Calvin private property and business were regulated according to the Consistory's interpretation of Scripture.[8]

For instance, in 1557 the tinsmiths petitioned the Consistory to prevent foreign tinsmiths from selling their products in Geneva. They argued that the foreign products, of inferior workmanship, could be sold at lower prices. (In Geneva of 1557, of the 228 metalworkers, one-third were goldsmiths.) Standards were established for the incoming refugees (who were entering Geneva almost daily). An elected industrial body called the Petit Conseil devised a set of metallurgical standards that the immigrants had to meet in order to ply their trade.[9]

As for usury, Calvin said that "it would be desirable that usury was erased from the face of this earth and its name unknown. But because this is impossible, one must give way to the common good."[10] He regarded chiliasm as a *horrendum dictu delirium*, as another of the religious fantasies for which Anabaptist radicals were known. (The Anabaptists derived their chiliasm from the Hussites and the Taborites of Bohemia.)[11]

EXAMPLES OF SOCIAL INFRACTIONS

Some crimes listed in 1562 were ridiculous—two Catholic peasants blamed the high prices at a market on the Genevan pastors. Two peasants from the Alps were arrested for selling cabbages at a suspiciously low price.[12] In 1562, thirty-nine trials were for

---

8. W. Fred Graham, *The Constructive Revolutionary—John Calvin and His Socio-Economic Impact* (Atlanta: John Knox Press, 1971), p. 144.

9. William C. Innes, *Social Concern in Calvin's Geneva* (Allison Park, P. A.: Pickwich Publications, 1983), p. 228.

10. *Commentaries*, Deuteronomy 23:29.

11. Willem Balke, trans. William Heynen, *Calvin and the Anabaptist Radicals* (Grand Rapids: William B. Eerdmans Publishing Company, 1981); *Commentaries*, 1 Thessalonians 4:17.

12. E. William Monter, "Crime and Punishment in Calvin's Geneva,"

immorality alone—including adultery, rape, and fornication, and forty other trials were over theft or trafficking in stolen goods. Twenty-one trials concerned professional infractions; one was the trial of a printer who published an unlicensed edition of the *Institutes*. The remainder of trials for that year ranged from usury to slander to homosexuality.[13] In 1562, the rate was 197 trials, or one per hundred of the population. In 1552, when Geneva had about 14,000 inhabitants, the 79 trials was a rate of one per 175.[14]

EXAMPLES OF SANCTIONS

Genevan magistrates passed the sentence of death on three rapists, two murderers, three thieves, two sodomites, and two alleged witches. A goldsmith from Lyon was beheaded for counterfeiting; other people were condemned for witchcraft, theft, adultery, fornication, heresy, treason, slander, and a riotous household. Trials that led to capital punishment or banishment accounted for fewer than one fourth. The majority of trials ended in a fine or imprisonment and a bread and water diet. The printer who published the unlicensed version of the *Institutes* was fined 100 ecus, paid to Calvin's brother Antione and the deacons of the Geneva hospital. The usual punishment for fornication was three days imprisonment on bread and water. Whipping or a time in the stocks was for sundry offenses, such as the woman who threw her child down in the street and cursed him (two hours in the stocks); a man who insulted his mother was sentenced to three hours. Those convicted of swearing, or of "arrogance" and "rebellion," had to recant in public.[15]

Enforcing Morality in Early Modern Europe (London, 1987), p. 283.

13. E. William Monter, "Crime and Punishment in Calvin's Geneva," *Enforcing Morality in Early Modern Europe*, p. 283.

14. E. William Monter, "Crime and Punishment in Calvin's Geneva," *Enforcing Morality in Early Modern Europe*, p. 282.

15. E. William Monter, "Crime and Punishment in Calvin's Geneva," *Enforcing Morality in Early Modern Europe*, p. 284.

Some court orders seem outlandish by our standards. One mother-in-law was barred from dining at her son-in-law's home because of her noisy, incessant quarreling. When a miller accused of professional infractions was unwilling to confess to wrongdoing even after imprisonment in irons, he was ordered to attend Catechism. One unfortunate peasant accidentally killed a child by running the child over with his cart, out of a bad conscience confessing, though the child's parents never sued him. The peasant was sentenced to a public penance and ordered to attend sermons for a full year.[16]

CONCLUSION

Calvin's social theory dominated the Genevan Consistory, the policymaking organ of the body politic. Calvin derived his social theory from the Bible. Public policy evolved through five phases—the Bible, Calvin's exegesis, Calvin's social theory, the Consistory's policy making, and the Consistory's recommendations to the councils for legislation. In our modern era of Western democracies, the *vox dei* has been replaced by the *vox populi*—from the people social theory derives, and social theory drives the lawmaking process.

---

16. E. William Monter, "Crime and Punishment in Calvin's Geneva," *Enforcing Morality in Early Modern Europe*, pp. 284–285.

COMMON POLITICAL THEMES AMONG CALVIN'S FELLOW REFORMERS

VARIOUS LUTHERANS

In 1536, Luther, Melancthon, Bugenhagen, Amsdorf, Jonas, and Cruciger signed a document contending, "In this case we conclude that every prince is responsible for maintaining and protecting Christians and their lawful, external worship against all unlawful powers; just as every prince is also responsible for protecting his pious subjects against all unlawful powers in regard to worldly affairs.[1] The difference between this and the Calvinist approach is that the latter proposes revolution, while the former suggests a much more limited obligation to protest.[2]

FRANCIS TURRETIN

Francis Turretin sees political-legal theology as evidence of God's covenant with mankind, the covenant itself a many-layered structure of divine and human relationships. His analysis of the covenant is in three parts: Turretin saw that God's covenant affected

---

1. Carlos M. N. Eire, *War Against the Idols—The Reformation of Worship from Erasmus to Calvin* (Cambridge: Cambridge University Press, 1986), p. 286.

2. W. D. J. Cargill Thompson, "Luther and the Right of Resistance to the Emperor," in *Church, Society, and Politics*, Derek Baker, ed. (Oxford, 1975), p. 161; Cynthia Grant Shoenberger, "The Development of the Lutheran Theory of Resistance: 1523–1530," *Sixteenth Century Journal*, 8:76 (1977).

relationships between humans. Humans who experience it relate with those of the same disposition, at a synergistic level. Hence, the covenant has a "dipleuric" human aspect.

Secondly, Turretin sees the covenant as existing between God and believers, where both interact on the spiritual plane; as God disposes, man proposes. The covenant made at Sinai is synergistic, according to Turretin. Last of all, Turretin sees God's covenant as a monergistic act, whereby God enters an eternal relationship with mankind. In this respect the covenant is irrevocable because it is a singular act of God (e. g. Jeremiah 31:31–34).[3]

Turretin calls the synergistic covenant the "covenant of works," and this is attended to by Christ. Hence, it represents the monergistic aspect of God's covenant, since Christ demonstrates the synergism linking the divine to mankind. Turretin explains how in Christ the covenant of human works and the covenant of divine grace combine: "Thus what was demanded of us in the covenant of works, is fulfilled by Christ in the covenant of grace. And thus in sweet harmony the law and the Gospel meet together in the Covenant of grace."[4]

PETER MARTYR VERMIGLI

In his *Loci Communes*, Vermigli's discussion of the Book of Judges includes examples of legitimate resistance, including Roman, Danish, and English (chronicled by Polydore Vergil).[5] Here is Vermigli's theology of resistance, showing how subordinate magistrates are to resist superiors for the Reformation's sake:

3. Stephen R. Spencer, "Francis Turretin's Concept of the Covenant of Nature," in *Later Calvinism—International Perspectives* (Ann Arbor: Edwards Brothers, 1994), p. 79ff.; Francois Turrettini, *Institutio Theologiae Elencticae* (Phillipsburg, N. J.: Presbyterian and Reformed Publishing, 1992), 12.12.22.

4. Francois Turrettini, *Institutio Theologiae Elencticae* (Phillipsburg, N. J.: Presbyterian and Reformed Publishing, 1992), 12.12.22.

5. B. A. Gerrish, "The Function of Law in the Political Thought of Peter Martyr Vermigli—Reformatio Prerennis: Essays on Calvin and the Reformation in Honor of Ford Lewis Battles," *Church and Society in Reformation Europe* (London: Variorum Reprints, 1985), p. 165.

> But thou wilt say: by what law do inferior princes resist either the emperor, or kings, or else public wealths [republics], when they defend the sincere religion and true faith? I answer by the law of the Emperor, or by the law of the king, or by the law of the public wealth. For they [the inferior princes] are chosen of emperors, kings, and public wealths as helpers to rule, whereby justice may more and more flourish. And therefore were they ordained according to the office committed unto them, rightly, justly, and godly to govern the public wealth. Wherefore they do according to their duty, when in cause of religion they resist the higher power.[6]

Vermigli argues that a sociopolitical contract exists between elected officials and their constituents. If officials violate their "covenants and promises" to their constituents, the constituents have the right to compel their performance by whatever means necessary, including war:

> There be others in the commonwealth, which in place and dignity are inferior unto princes, and yet in very deed do elect the superior power, and by certain laws do govern the commonwealth, as this day we see done by the Electors of the Empire, and perhaps the same is done in other kingdoms. To these undoubtedly if the prince perform not his covenants and promises, it is lawful to contradict and bring him into order, and by force to compel him to perform the conditions and covenants which he had promised, and that by war when it cannot otherwise be done.[7]

---

6. B. A. Gerrish, "The Function of Law in the Political Thought of Peter Martyr Vermigli—Reformatio Prerennis: Essays on Calvin and the Reformation in Honor of Ford Lewis Battles," *Church and Society in Reformation Europe* (London: Variorum Reprints, 1985), p. 164 citing Vermigli's commentary on Judges 1:36.

7. *Loci Communes* IV: 20, 13; B. A. Gerrish, "The Function of Law in the Political Thought of Peter Martyr Vermigli—Reformatio Prerennis: Essays on Calvin and the Reformation in Honor of Ford Lewis Battles," *Church and Society in Reformation Europe* (London: Variorum Reprints, 1985), p. 165.

Theodore Beza

Theodore Beza's work, *On the Right of Magistrates* (1574), argues for a constitutionalist state doctrine. To the question of the treatise, "Should magistrates as well as God be unconditionally obeyed?" he answers:

> The only will that is a perpetual and immutable criterion of justice is the will of the one God and none other. Hence him alone we are obliged to obey without exception. Princes too would have to be obeyed implicitly if they were always the voice of God's commandments. But since the opposite too often happens, an exception is imposed upon obedience, when their commands are irreligious or iniquitous. Irreligious commands are those which order us to do what the First Table of God's Law forbids, or forbid us to do what it commands.[8]

Accordingly, Beza envisioned the Table of God's Law as a constitutional authority over the Christian state.

JOHANNES PHILLIPE DU PLESSIS-MORNAY

Writing his *Vindiciae contra turannos* in 1579, Phillipe du Plessis-Mornay establishes his political theory regarding covenants with God. According to Mornay, regardless of their political history, rulers are obliged to God. Rulers are obliged to enter and maintain a covenant with God for the sake of maintaining order, especially that related to worship. The governed are also obliged to enter a covenant with God to maintain order and true worship. Each party, even an absolute monarch, has a responsibility to the nation's covenant with itself and God: "The covenant remains the same; the stipulations are unaltered; and there are the same penalties if these

---

8. Theodore Beza, *Du Droit des Magistrats sur les Subjects. Traite Tres-necessarie in ce Temps, pour Advertir de Leur Devoir, Tant les Magistrats que les Subjects: Publiee par Ceux de Magdenbourg, l'an MDL; et Maintenant Reveu et Augumente de Plusieurs et Exemples*, as cited by Carlos M. N. Eire, *War Against the Idols—The Reformation of Worship from Erasmus to Calvin* (Cambridge: Cambridge University Press, 1986), p. 297.

are not fulfilled, as well as the same God, omnipotent, avenging perfidy."[9]

Plessis-Mornay asks "Are subjects bound to obey princes if their orders contradict the law of God?" answering with: "If the vassal does keep the fealty he swore, his fief is forfeited and he is legally deprived of all prerogatives. So also with the king. If he neglects God, if he goes over to His enemies and is guilty of felony towards God, his kingdom is forfeited of right and is often lost in fact."[10] He explains his view of the relationship between "a religious people" and their magistrate: "A religious people not only will restrain a prince in the act of doing violence to God's law, but will from the beginning prevent gradual changes arising from his guilt or negligence, for the true worship of God may be slowly corrupted over extended periods of time. Moreover, they will not only refuse to tolerate crimes committed against God's majesty in public, but will constantly strive to remove all occasions for such crime.... It is, then, not only lawful for Israel to resist a king who overturns the Law and the Church of God, but if they do not do so, they are guilty of the same crime and subject to the same penalty."[11]

Peter Martyr supports Plessis-Mornay in his 1554 Commentary on Judges: "as idolatry is the cause of captivity, pestilence and famine, and the overthrowing of publique wealthes, shall it not pertaine unto the Magistrate to repress it, and to keep the true and sound religion?"[12] According to Mornay, the individual subject was responsible to his own person and body, "which is God's Temple," just as a person's life must be pure and fit dwelling place for God's Spirit.[13] The magistrate, however, had great responsibil-

9. Carlos M. N. Eire, *War Against the Idols—The Reformation of Worship from Erasmus to Calvin* (Cambridge: Cambridge University Press, 1986), p. 299.

10. Mornay, *Vindiciae*, translated in Julian H. Franklin, *Constitutionalism and Resistance in the Sixteenth Century: Three Treatises by Hotman, Beza and Mornay* (New York: Pegasus, 1969), p. 143.

11. *Vindiciae*, p. 149.

12. Peter Martyr, *Commentary on Judges*, 1564 ed., fols. 266v–267r.

13. Mornay, *Vindiciae*, p. 155.

ity: "When we speak of the people collectively, we mean those who receive authority from the people, that is, the magistrates below the king who have been elected by the people or established in some other way."[14] The duty of the magistrate is the make sure the "temple of God is not ruined or polluted."[15]

If a king drives people to idolatry, Plessis-Mornay advises two different courses of action depending on circumstances. When magistrates intervene against the king over this, then the people of God should "obey and follow and use all their energy and zeal as soldiers on the side of God to support these holy enterprises." Magistrates may choose not to rebel, or resist, or submit. If they choose to rebel, however, then the people must rebel also. In circumstances where the king drives subjects to idolatry and the magistrates do not resist the king, believers must go elsewhere to another country. Author Eire reminds us that "under no condition does Plessis-Mornay sanction an uprising that is not led by the magistracy."[16] Local magistracy, however, when other magistracies did not resist persecution, could "at least drive idolatry beyond their borders" or even secede from the larger body politic, if necessary.[17] Although the Church is not to be enlarged by violence or military power, by violence or military power the Church can be defended.[18]

JOHANNES COCCEIUS

Johannes Cocceius (1603–99) contends that the Decalogue expresses God's immutable natural laws, and that these transcend

---

14. Mornay, *Vindiciae*, p. 149.

15. Carlos M. N. Eire, *War Against the Idols—The Reformation of Worship from Erasmus to Calvin* (Cambridge: Cambridge University Press, 1986), p. 300.

16. Carlos M. N. Eire, *War Against the Idols—The Reformation of Worship from Erasmus to Calvin* (Cambridge: Cambridge University Press, 1986), p. 300.

17. Mornay, *Vindiciae*, p. 157.

18. Mornay, *Vindiciae*, p. 156.

all biblical revelation.[19] This Decalogue summarizes all aspects of obedience.[20] To Cocceius, the monadic covenant divaricates into two compacts, the first made with the pristine Adam. "The covenant consists of stipulatio, promissio, adstipulatio, and ius petendum or restipulatio. (*Stipulatio* refers to God's demand for a guarantee from a prospective debtor. *Adstipulatio* is the concordance of an associate in a stipulation; *restipulatio* is the demand for a counter-guarantee.) Conditional upon Adam's behavior in the Garden of Eden, probation, God would reward Adam and his offspring with full *communio atque amicitia*.[21] Since this was imprinted on Adam by the divine creative hand, this natural law was his chief concern. Fallen mankind is a remnant of the original legal arrangement between God and Adam.[22] The tree of knowledge, a signum representing Adam's temptation, was also the symbol of this covenant.[23] If Adam resisted temptation, then he would be justly rewarded, having signified his obedience, and thus honoring the covenant. The covenant was not an exchange between equals, however.[24] God, of his own resolve, says his response is determined by Adam's actions. He reserves the right to judge Adam's descendants accordingly, for that is part of the covenant, a contingency of Adam's violation, his disobedience.[25]

Adam's period of probation in Eden was not a velleity of divine caprice, but an act of propriety and rectitude toward his creation. By giving Adam volition towards righteousness, he does

---

19. Johannes Cocceius, *Summa Doctrinae de Foedere et Testamento Dei*, 13.

20. Johannes Cocceius, *Summan Theologiae ex Scripturis Repetita* (Genevae, 1665), LIV, p. 10; Johannes Cocceius, *Summa Doctrinae de Foedere et Testamento Dei* (Lugduni Batavorum, 1660), p. 338 (XXXV).

21. Johannes Cocceius, *Summa Theologiae*, XXII, 17, 18, 19.

22. Johannes Cocceius, *Summa Doctrinae*, 8, 71.

23. Johannes Cocceius, *Summa Theologiae*, 19.

24. There is no arrearage, congruity, or proration between God and Adam, but God, of his own autarkic resolve, astricts himself ex pacto to respond to his creature's comportment. God sees Adam as the caput of his created stock. Johannes Cocceius, *Summa Doctrinae*, 41.

25. Johannes Cocceius, *Summa Theologiae*, XXX, 2.

not pervert Adam's free will; Adam is still free to choose evil over good.[26] God's interjecting a volitional appetite into Adam for righteousness does not invert Adam's inherent free will, the ability to choose evil and as well as good.[27] Embedded in the pristine Adam was a craving to adore and worship God,[28] but in violating the creation pact, he lapsed into spiritual oblivion.[29] Under a New Covenant, God promises to save His believers.[30]

Because of the nature of his obedience, Christ earned righteousness for all God's elect[31]:

> The only distinction of paramountcy as far as the deposit of salvation is concerned involved those who have been secluded from any revelatory attestation of that blessed hope. God simply does not provide credence for such a belief from natural illumination. Although the long-suffering and mercy of God are intimated naturally to man, even His ability to justify the sinner, the exact modus operandi in the covenant of grace, being solely a product of good pleasure, is unveiled through a special transcendent word alone."[32]

Cocceius sees Genesis as providing the foundation of the covenant between God and his people.[33] Genesis 3:15 records the original new covenant God made with Adam.[34]

---

26. Johannes Cocceius, *Summa Theologiae*, XIV, 7, 8.

27. Johannes Cocceius, *Summa Doctrinae*, 43.

28. Johannes Cocceius, *Summa Doctrinae*, 43.

29. Johannes Cocceius, *Summa Doctrinae*, 42, 76.

30. Johannes Cocceius, *Summa Doctrinae*, 43, 86.

31. Christ merited righteousness ex condigno. Johannes Cocceius, *Summa Doctrinae* 77–78, 103, 350.

32. Stephen Strehle, *Calvinism, Federalism, and Scholasticism—A Study of the Reformed Doctrine of Covenant* (New York: Lang, 1988), pp. 230–31.

33. Johannes Cocceius, *Summa Doctinrae*, 289.

34. Cocceius saw the original Verbum Testamenti of Genesis 3:15 as transmitted without clear codification *ex compacto*. The Verbum Testamenti was revitalized periodically through the auspices of the Patriarchs. Johannes Cocceius, *Summa Theologiae*, II, 1141; XK, 24–26.

Under Moses, the people of Israel were not called to action by an outmoded covenant, but one that God established for them as a covenant of grace.[35] The deposition of this covenant includes two testaments, one earthly in orientation, and one heavenly in orientation.[36] To Cocceius, the Decalogue belongs to the covenant of grace because it reveals divine holiness and the pattern of people's obedience.[37]

JOHANNES CLOPPENBURG

Cloppenburg's ideas come from God's *oikonomia* (God's rule of the house, meaning all mankind). This *oikonomia* is not confined, delimited, or constricted to professing believers; rather it is universal, regardless of religious persuasion, over each and every person. Adam's responsibility was as a *perens ac stirps*, to the entire race,[38] and thus responsible for conserving natural law. (This included a commission to multiply, and to dominate the whole earth, and to refrain from eating the forbidden fruit).[39]

According to Cloppenburg, God's obligation to bless Adam arises from his covenant, because he is compelled to become mankind's debtor.[40] (The reward for obeying the covenant obedience is *libarae voluntatis*.).[41] In *Disputationes Theologicae XI de Foedere Dei et Testamento veteri & novo*, Cloppenburg acknowledges that the first *oeconomia* extends from Adam to Moses, preserved through oral tradition, and subject to periodic reinvigoration by

35. Johannes Cocceius, *Summa Doctrinae*, 338 (XXVIII).

36. Two patria, one on earth in Canaan and one in heaven. Johannes Cocceius, *Summa Doctrinae*, 330 (XXVIII).

37. Johannes Cocceius, *Summa Theologiae*, LIV, 14.

38. Johannes Cloppenburg, *Disputationes Theologicae XI de Foedere Dei et Testamento veteri & novo*, I, 2.

39. Johannes Cloppenburg, *Disputationes Theologicae XI de Foedere Dei et Testamento veteri & novo*, I, 23–25.

40. Johannes Cloppenburg, *Disputationes Theologicae XI de Foedere Dei et Testamento veteri & novo*, I, 17; II, 3.

41. Johannes Cloppenburg, *Disputationes Theologicae XI de Foedere Dei et Testamento veteri & novo*, I, 17; II, 3.

such Patriarchs as Noah and Abraham. The succeeding revelations are recorded in writing and lead to a knowledge of Christ.[42]

WILLIAM AMES

The A. S. P. Woodhouse discussion of William Ames' (1576–1633) work *Conscience* includes Ames' view of natural law, namely the divine and human. Ames makes a clear distinction between right natural and right positive divine law: "Right natural is that which is apprehended to be fit to be done or avoided, out of the natural instinct of natural light; or that which is at least deduced from the natural light by evident consequence. So that this right partly consists of practical principles known by nature, and partly of conclusions deduced from these principles." By definition, "the divine positive right is a right added to the natural by some special revelation of God." Ames equates the right natural with "natural law" and "eternal law,"[43] as he explains: "the natural and positive divine right differ in this: that the positive is mutable and various according to God's good pleasure (for that which was heretofore in the Judaical church is different from that which is in the Christian church); but the right natural is always the same and like itself, and for this reason also it is called the law eternal."[44]

Ames contends that all aspects of moral law belong under the law of nature, except for celebrating the Sabbath, determined by the Fourth Commandment, and come from positive law. Ames argues that the moral law and the law of nature are contiguous, though he does not indicate clearly whether he means which day is the Sabbath or that only one day a week is for this purpose:

42. Johannes Cloppenburg, I, 18; III, 30; VIII, 4; IX, 17; V, 22, 31–32; Stephen Strehle, *Calvinism, Federalism, and Scholasticism—A Study of the Reformed Doctrine of Covenant* (New York: Lang, 1988), pp. 219ff.

43. A.S.P. Woodhouse, "Ames on the Law of Nature," *Puritanism and Liberty—Being the Army Debates (1647–9)* from the Clarke Manuscripts with Supplementary Documents (London: J. M. Dent, 1938), p. 187.

44. A.S.P. Woodhouse, "Ames on the Law of Nature," *Puritanism and Liberty—Being the Army Debates (1647–9)* from the Clarke Manuscripts with Supplementary Documents, p. 187.

COMMON POLITICAL THEMES AMONG CALVIN'S FELLOW REFORMERS

> For first, we meet with nothing in them which concerneth not all nations at all times, so that these precepts do not respect any particular sort of men, but even nature itself. Secondly, nothing is contained in them which is not very necessary to human nature for the attaining of its end. Thirdly, there is nothing in them which is not so grounded upon right reason but it may be solidly defended and maintained by human discourse; nothing but wrath may be well enjoined from clear reason. Fourthly, all things contained in them are for the substance approved, even of the more understanding sort of the heathen. Fifthly, they all much conduce to the benefit of mankind in this present life; insomuch that if all these precepts were duly answered, there would be no need of any other human laws or constitutions.[45]

Ames divides Old Testament law into three categories:

> That is properly termed the Judicial which is about judgments or any politic matters thereto belonging, that was called the Ceremonial Law which was ceremonies, and that the Moral Law which was about manners and civil duties. That Judicial Law which was given by Moses to the Israelites as proper only to them, was a most exact determination and accommodation of that people.[46]

He restricts the use of Israelite judicial law to the Jews:

> To the Israelites therefore in respect of the use, it was of like nature with those good civil laws among other nations; but in respect of authority, which from God, the immediate giver, it received, it was of much more perfection than any. This law belongeth not to Christians under the title of a law especially obliging them, or in its due

---

45. A. S. P. Woodhouse, "Ames on the Law of Nature," *Puritanism and Liberty—Being the Army Debates (1647-9)* from the Clarke Manuscripts with Supplementary Documents (London: J. M. Dent, 1938), p. 190.

46. A. S. P. Woodhouse, "Ames on the Law of Nature," *Puritanism and Liberty—Being the Army Debates (1647-9)* from the Clarke Manuscripts with Supplementary Documents, pp. 191–92.

proportion to it, it doth always exhibit unto use the best determination of the law of nature.[47]

And:

Those laws were properly termed Judicial, which being not ceremonial, had some singular respect to the people of the Jews, so that the whole reason and ground of them was constituted in some particular condition of that nation."[48]

Ames contends that judicial law is moral:

But where the special intrinsical and proper reason of the law is moral, there it always follows that the law itself must needs be moral. Those laws, therefore, which are usually reckoned among the judicial, and yet in their nature bear no singular respect to the condition of the Jews more than of any other people, those are all of the moral and natural laws which are common to all nations.[49]

JOHN GOODWIN

John Goodwin, the Arminian brother of Puritan Thomas Goodwin, argues for the right of the people to elect representatives to constitute a Parliament and to form an army. Goodwin argues that "the authority and power of the people (or rather the present exercise and execution of this power) to act for their own preservation and well-being in every kind, was as well formally, and according to the ceremony of the law, as really, and according to the true

---

47. A. S. P. Woodhouse, "Ames on the Law of Nature," *Puritanism and Liberty—Being the Army Debates (1647-9)* from the Clarke Manuscripts with Supplementary Documents (London: J. M. Dent, 1938), p. 191.

48. A. S. P. Woodhouse, "Ames on the Law of Nature," *Puritanism and Liberty—Being the Army Debates (1647-9)* from the Clarke Manuscripts with Supplementary Documents, p. 191.

49. A. S. P. Woodhouse, "Ames on the Law of Nature," *Puritanism and Liberty—Being the Army Debates (1647-9)* from the Clarke Manuscripts with Supplementary Documents, p. 191.

intentions and desires of the people, vested in Parliament."[50] One unknown author (perhaps John Goodwin), wrote "An Exhortation to the Bishops to Deal Brotherly with Their Brethren," in making an earnest plea addresses to the bishops. The preface to this work exemplifies the allusions that are common in such writings. In most respects it is similar in style and function to Calvin's discussions:

> Why blame you not Isaiah, that terms the ministers of his age, blind watchmen, dumb dogs, greedy dogs? What say you to Jeremiah, who names pastors beasts? How will you deal with Ezekiel, that nameth the Prophets conspirators, greedy raveners, and devourers like roaring lions? How shall Hosea be intreated, that compareth the Priests to them that secretly lie in wait for a man? What shall become of Micah, that can vouchsafe to give them no better names than deceivers and biters of the Lord's people with their teeth. But how will you handle Zechariah, who in vehemence of spirit calls them idols?[51]

This unknown author equated the bishopric with tyranny.

SAMUEL RUTHERFORD

Samuel Rutherford confirms the Puritan Presbyterian principles regarding resistance to civil government; according to A. S. P. Woodhouse, Rutherford's *Lex Rex* was a Puritan response to John Maxwell's *Sacrosancta regum majestas*: "And wherever God appointed a king, he never appointed him absolute and a sole independent agent, but joined always with him judges, who were no

---

50. A. S. P. Woodhouse, *Puritanism and Liberty—Being the Army Debates (1647-9)* from the Clarke Manuscripts with Supplementary Documents (London: J. M. Dent, 1938), p. 214.

51. W.H. Frere and C. E. Douglas, eds., *Puritan Manifestoes—A Study of the Origin of the Puritan Revolt* (New York: Franklin, 1972), pp. 58-59; for an excellent historical survey of the Puritan Revolution, see Geoffrey F. Nuttall, *Visible Saints: The Congregational Way, 1640-1660* (Oxford: Basil Blackwell, 1957), "Historical Introduction," pp. 1-42.

less to judge according to the Law of God (2 Chron. 19:6) than the king (Deut. 17:15).[52]

Rutherford refrains from saying outright that monarchical and aristocratic governments are not of God, or that representative democracies are. Rather, Rutherford asserts that "all the three be from God, even as single life and marriage are both the lawful ordinances of God," adding that none of the three forms of government is of human invention: "Nor are we to think that aristocracy and democracy are either unlawful ordinances or men's inventions, or that those societies which want monarchy do therefore live in sins."[53]

The people chose kings, according to Rutherford: "Let Royalists show us any act of God making David king, save this act of the people as God's instrument transferred the power, and God by them in the same act transferred the power, and in the same they chose the person. The power is the people's, radically, naturally. And God hath revealed (in Deuteronomy 17:14–15) the way of regulating the act of choosing governors and kings, which is a special mean of defending and protecting themselves; and the people is principally the subject and fountain of royal power, as a fountain is of water. I shall not call a fountain God's instrument to give water, as all creatures are his instruments."[54]

This example, cited by A. S. P. Woodhouse from *Lex Rex* (1644) sees as individual the quest for Reformation:

> The Presbyterians hold (I believe with warrant of God's word): if the king refuse to reform religion, the inferior judges and assembly of godly pastors and other church officers may reform; if the king will . . . do his duty in purging the House of the Lord, may not Elijah and the

---

52. A. S. P. Woodhouse, *Puritanism and Liberty—Being the Army Debates (1647-9) from the Clarke Manuscripts with Supplementary Documents*, p. 202.

53. A. S. P. Woodhouse, *Puritanism and Liberty—Being the Army Debates (1647-9) from the Clarke Manuscripts with Supplementary Documents* (London: J. M. Dent, 1938), p. 202.

54. A. S. P. Woodhouse, *Puritanism and Liberty—Being the Army Debates (1647-9) from the Clarke Manuscripts with Supplementary Document*, p. 212.

people do their duty and cast out Baal's priests? Reformation of religion is a personal act that belongeth to all, even to any one private person according to his place.[55]

Agreeing with Calvin, Rutherford believes that kings should not be absolute because God intends their rule to be connected with judges: "And wherever God appointed a king, he never appointed him absolute and a sole independent agent, but joined always with him judges, who were no less to judge according to the Law of God (2 Chronicles 19:6) than the king (Deuteronomy 17:15)."[56] Rutherford believes that subjects making the monarch a constitutional monarch, saying that the covenant between a king and his subjects requires the king to answer to his subjects, citing, for example, 2 Samuel 5:3 ("So all the elders of Israel came to the king to Hebron, and King David made a covenant with them in Hebron before the Lord, and they anointed David king over Israel"), 1 Chronicles 11:3 ("And David made a covenant with them before the Lord, and they anointed David king over Israel, according to the word of the Lord by Samuel"), and 2 Chronicles 23:3 ("And all the congregation made a covenant with the king, Joash, in the house of God").[57] As Rutherford explains:

> We are all by nature free. As domestic society is natural, being grounded upon nature's instinct, so politic society is voluntary, being grounded on the consent of me. And so politic society is natural *in radice*, in the root, and voluntary and free *in modo*, in the manner of their union; and the scripture cleareth to us that a king is made by the free consent of the people (Deuteronomy 17:15), and so not by nature. What is from the womb, and so natural, is

---

55. A. S. P. Woodhouse, "Ames on the Law of Nature," *Puritanism and Liberty—Being the Army Debates (1647–9)* from the Clarke Manuscripts with Supplementary Documents, p. 199.

56. A. S. P. Woodhouse, "Principles of Resistance," *Puritanism and Liberty—Being the Army Debates (1647–9)* from the Clarke Manuscripts with Supplementary Documents (London: J. M. Dent, 1938), p. 207.

57. A. S. P. Woodhouse, "Principles of Resistance," *Puritanism and Liberty—Being the Army Debates (1647–9)* from the Clarke Manuscripts with Supplementary Documents, p. 207.

eternal and agreeth to all societies of men; but a monarchy agreeth not to all societies of men; but a monarchy agreeth not to all societies of men; for many hundred year de facto there was not a king, till Nimrod's time the world being governed by families, and till Moses' history we find no institution for kings (Genesis 7). And the numerous multiplication of mankind did occasion monarchs. Otherwise fatherly government being the first, and measure of the rest, must be the best.[58]

To Rutherford, the power to make kings comes from God, but through the people.[59]

JOHN OWEN AND JOHN LOCKE

Both Owen and Locke were disciples of John Calvin. John Owen and John Locke first met while Locke was a student at Christ Church, Oxford, from 1656 to 1660. From 1651 to 1660, Owen was dean of Christ Church and from 1652 to 1657, vice-chancellor of Oxford University. Although the precise extent of Owen's contact with Locke is not known, both H. R. Fox Bourne and Peter Toon suppose that Owen had a dramatic influence on Locke in the matter of religious toleration.[60] Owen argued for toleration even while the Westminster Assembly was in session. In 1646, Owen argued: "I never knew one contend earnestedly for a toleration of dissenters, but was so himself; nor any for their suppression, but were themselves of the persuasion which prevails."[61]

---

58. A. S. P. Woodhouse, "Principles of Resistance," *Puritanism and Liberty—Being the Army Debates (1647-9)* from the Clarke Manuscripts with Supplementary Documents (London: J. M. Dent, 1938), p. 207.

59. A. S. P. Woodhouse, "Principles of Resistance," *Puritanism and Liberty—Being the Army Debates (1647-9)* from the Clarke Manuscripts with Supplementary Documents, p. 212.

60. H.R. Fox Bourne, *The Life of John Locke* (London: Henry S. King & Co., 1876), vol. 1, pp. 72–79; Peter Toon, *God's Statesman: The Life and Work of John Owen, Pastor, Educator, Theologian* (Exeter: Paternoster Press, 1971), pp. 60–63.

61. William H. Gould, ed., *The Works of John Owen* (London: Banner of

Locke's four manuscript drafts of "Essay on Toleration" date to 1667, but none indicates either the day or month. Owen's treatises dating to 1667 may have been read by Locke before he published his soon-to-be-popular diatribe against religious persecution. Locke argues that matters of doctrine and worship, which "in themselves concern not government and society at all, have an absolute and universal right to toleration."[62]

According to author J. Wayne Baker, Calvin and the Congregationalist Puritans, of whom Owen was a luminary, agreed that ecclesiastical discipline should be exercised by the local congregation (meaning in the local assembly) led by their body of elders.[63] Baker says that Calvin and the Congregationalists believed that these local congregations, as led by elected elders, should enforce ecclesiastical law, that is, the New Testament law of liberty in the context of the particular local church.[64]

JOHN KNOX

Knox's Spiritual Development, the Reformation in Scotland, and Knox's Questions About Its Course

Knox's boldness in prosecuting the Reformation in Scotland derives from a spiritual development acquired in extremity, since for nineteen months he served as a galley slave for his part in an insurrection at St. Andrews in 1547.[65] The work of the academy

---

Truth Trust, 1967), 8:55, 58–69. For an excellent survey of Owen' s Calvinistic theology, see Richard M. Hawkes, "The Logic of Grace in John Owen, D.D.: An Analysis, Exposition, and Defense of John Owen's Puritan Theology of Grace," (Unpublished Ph.D. dissertation, Westminster Theological Seminary, 1987).

62. Fox Bourne, ed., *The Life of John Locke (1876)*, 1:174–94.

63. J. Wayne Baker, "Church, State, and Toleration: John Locke and Calvin's Heirs in England, 1644–89)" in *Later Calvinism—International Perspectives* (Ann Arbor: Edwards Brothers, 1994), p. 531.

64. Calvin, *Institutes*, 4.20.

65. Carlos M.N. Eire, *War Against the Idols—The Reformation of Worship from Erasmus to Calvin* (Cambridge: Cambridge University Press, 1986), pp. 276–79; John Knox, "Certain Questions Concerning Obedience to Lawful

CALVIN THE MAGISTRATE

at Geneva thoroughly engaged Knox, for it is here that he learned about Christ:

> I neither fear nor ashame to say, [Geneva] is the most perfect school of Christ that ever was in earth since the days of the Apostles. In other places, I confess Christ to be truly preached; but manners and religion so sincerely reformed, I have not yet seen in any other place.[66]

When the theology and politics of Geneva were exported to a new society, including Scotland, the social fabric invariably changed in two ways: religious attacks upon idolatry resulted in iconoclasm and anti-clericalism, and citizens formulated political postures of resistance and in some cases outright rebellion.[67] Under Knox's leadership, in Scotland the Calvinist revolution resulted in the entire country's rising up against idols.[68] Unlike England, where the growth of Protestantism was erratic, depending on the monarch, Scotland took to the Calvinist revolution en masse. Eventually, the Calvinistic Puritan revolution engulfed England, Wales, and all of Ireland by 1640.[69]

Knox's discussion centers around four questions. First, is it necessary for God's people to obey a child-monarch? Second, does a woman have status to rule by divine right? Third, is it necessary for God's people to obey a magistrate who enforces idolatry and condemns the true religion? And fourth, to which faction should

---

Magistrates," in *The Works of John Knox*, D. Laing, ed. (6 vols., Edinburgh, 1846–64, reprinted, New York, 1966), vol. 3, pp. 217–26.

66. *The Works of John Knox*, vol. 4, p. 240.

67. Carlos M.N. Eire, *War Against the Idols—The Reformation of Worship from Erasmus to Calvin* (Cambridge: Cambridge University Press, 1986), pp. 278–79.

68. Carlos M.N. Eire, *War Against the Idols—The Reformation of Worship from Erasmus to Calvin* (Cambridge: Cambridge University Press, 1986), p. 281.

69. Carlos M.N. Eire, *War Against the Idols—The Reformation of Worship from Erasmus to Calvin* (Cambridge: Cambridge University Press, 1986), p. 281; for an overview of the iconoclasm in Scotland see Mary Paton Ramsey, *Calvin and Art, Considered in Relation to Scotland* (Edinburgh, 1938) and A.M. Renwick, *The Story of the Scottish Reformation* (London, 1960).

God's people adhere if godly men in political positions resist an idolatrous king through resort to violence? Seeking answers to these questions, Knox wrote Calvin for guidance.[70]

The Sources of Knox's Political Theology

Although Knox's thinking is derived almost entirely from the Old Testament, he looked for guidance to Calvin, Viret, and Bullinger to ascertain the proper analogy and application.[71] Regarding whether Christian citizens should rebel or not, Calvin replies that under no circumstances was it lawful to rise up in open rebellion against an idolatrous ruler. Calvin wrote a letter introducing Knox to Pierre Viret of Lausanne and Heinrich Bullinger of Zurich so the Knox could further inquire of them. Bullinger's response is that children and women can rule under divine providence and that God's people cannot rebel against providentially appointed rulers. Bullinger adds, however, "But the Lord will in his own time destroy unjust governments by his own people, to whom he will supply proper qualification for this purpose, as he formerly did to Jerubaal, and the Maccabees."[72]

Bullinger hedges about specifics, however, saying although Paul counsels submission (Romans 13:1–7); rebellion in specific circumstances is "very difficult to pronounce" and "it would be very stupid to state any definite conclusions."[73] Knox, for instance, in Admonition or Warning, writes in 1553–54 that it is the duty of

---

70. Carlos M.N. Eire, *War Against the Idols—The Reformation of Worship from Erasmus to Calvin* (Cambridge: Cambridge University Press, 1986), pp. 276–79; John Knox, *The Works of John Knox*, "Certain Questions Concerning Obedience to Lawful Magistrates," vol. 3, pp. 217–26.

71. Richard G. Kyle, *The Mind of John Knox* (Lawrence, Kansas, 1984).

72. Carlos M.N. Eire, *War Against the Idols—The Reformation of Worship from Erasmus to Calvin* (Cambridge: Cambridge University Press, 1986), pp. 277.

73. Carlos M.N. Eire, *War Against the Idols—The Reformation of Worship from Erasmus to Calvin* (Cambridge: Cambridge University Press, 1986), p. 277.

every "Civil Magistrate" to "slay all idolaters."[74] In May 31, 1554, Knox wrote to friends in England of his hope that God would "stir up on Jehu or other to execute his vengeance upon these bloodthirsty tyrants and obstinate idolaters."[75] Later, in July 1554, Knox prayed that God would provide a Phinehas, an Elijah, or a Jehu to topple Mary Tudor. Further, he repeated Jeremiah's exhortation that allowed for one to suspend obedience to princes and to obey the enemies of the state.[76]

Concerning whether a woman should rule, Knox turns to an illustration used by Karlstadt in 1525. Karlstadt said that Luther was like a child with a sword, and this the imperial Papacy had to remove, lest he hurt himself or others. Knox likens Mary to an abusive, sword-wielding parent, who has to be subdued lest the child be irreparably harmed.[77]

The Common Views of Knox, Goodman, and Ponet

Three adherents of the Reformation in Scotland—John Knox, Christopher Goodman and John Ponet—contend that God's people, like the Israelites of the Old Testament, are in covenant with God to defend true worship both by doctrinal persuasion

---

74. John Knox, *The Works of John Knox*, ed. David Laing, 6 vols. (1854-95; reprint ed., New York: AMS, 1966), 6:236; Richard L. Greaves, "Calvinism, Democracy, and the Political Thought of John Knox," *Calvinism in France, Netherlands, Scotland, and England, Articles on Calvin and Calvinism*, vol. 14, p. 207.

75. John Knox, *The Works of John Knox*, ed. David Laing, 6 vols. (1854-95; reprint ed., New York: AMS, 1966), 3:247; Richard L. Greaves, "Calvinism, Democracy, and the Political Thought of John Knox," *Calvinism in France, Netherlands, Scotland, and England, Articles on Calvin and Calvinism*, vol. 14, p. 207.

76. John Knox, *The Works of John Knox*, ed. David Laing, 6 vols. (1854-95; reprint ed., New York: AMS, 1966), 3:309, 312, 325-26.

77. W. Croft Dickinson, ed., *John Knox's History of the Reformation in Scotland* (2 vols., Edinburgh, 1949), vol. 2, pp. 13-20; Richard L. Greaves, *Theology and Revolution in the Scottish Reformation* (Grand Rapids: 1980), pp. 111-68.

COMMON POLITICAL THEMES AMONG CALVIN'S FELLOW REFORMERS

and political/military power.[78] This Scottish triumvirate argues that the magistracy, nobility and estates are commanded by God to execute all idolaters, including kings.[79] "First we may hereof justly conclude, that to obey man in any thing contrary to God, or his precepts though he be in highest authority, or never so orderly called there unto . . . is not obedience at all, but disobedience . . . there is no obedience against God which is not plain disobedience."[80] And:

> For what is King, Queen, or Emperor compared to God? Of the which we may justly conclude, that by the ordinance of God, no other kings or Rulers ought to be chosen to rule over us, but such as will seek his honor and glory, and will command and do nothing contrary to his Law . . . But if they will abuse his power, lifting themselves above God and above their brethren, to draw them to idolatrie, and to oppress them, and their

---

78. John Knox, *The First Blast of the Trumpet against the Monstrous Regiment of Women* (Geneva, 1558); John Knox, *Appellation to the Nobility and Estates of Scotland* (Geneva, 1558); Christopher Goodman, *How Superior Powers Ought to be Obeyed of Their Subjects, and Wherein They May Lawfully by God's Word Be Disobeyed and Resisted* (Geneva, 1558); John Ponet, *A Short Treatise of Politick Power* (Strassburg, 1556).

79. Carlos M.N. Eire, *War Against the Idols—The Reformation of Worship from Erasmus to Calvin* (Cambridge: Cambridge University Press, 1986), p. 301; Richard L. Greaves: "John Knox, the Reformed Tradition, and the Development of Resistance Theory," *Journal of Modern History*, 48: supplement (September 1976) and "Calvinism, Democracy and the Political Thought of John Knox," Occasional Papers of the American Society for Reformation Research, 1:81–91 (December, 1977); Robert Linder, "Pierre Viret and the Sixteenth-Century English Protestants," *Archiv fur Reformationsgeschichte*, 58: 149–70 (1976); Dan G. Danner, "Christopher Goodman and the English Protestant Tradition of Civil Disobedience," *Sixteenth Century Journal*, 8: 61–73 (1977); Leo F. Solt, "Revolutionay Calvinist Parties in England under Elizabeth I and Charles I," *Church History* 28: 234–9 (1958); Marvin Anderson, "Royal Idolatry: Peter Martyr and the Reformed Tradition," *Archiv fur Reformationsgeschichte*, 69: 157–20 (1978).

80. Christopher Goodman, Superior Powers (1958), cited in Edmund S. Morgan, *Puritan Political Ideas, 1558–1794* (Indianapolis, 1965), p. 2 and Carlos M.N. Eire, *War Against the Idols—The Reformation of Worship from Erasmus to Calvin* (Cambridge: Cambridge University Press, 1986), p. 302.

contrie: then are they no more to be obeyed in any commandments tending to that end.. . . . For the same God commanded Moyses to hang up all the capitaynes and heads of the people, for that by their example they made the people idolatrers also: he had no respect to their authoritie, because they were Rulers, but so muche the rather woulde he have them so sharplie punished, that is, hanged agaynst the sunne without mercy."[81]

Both Goodman and Knox contend that not only do the ruler's negative duties prevent harm to God's people, but also the positive, by rooting out evil and repudiating "all forms of idolatry and tyranny." It is the duty, therefore, of rulers to become Christians and actively, by force if necessary, enforce the law of God in their domains. Because each nation is in covenant with God, each citizen is obliged by a sacred duty not only to disobey passively but to actively resist and remove all idolatrous or tyrannical magistrates.[82] Failure to resist idolatrous rulers was covenantal disobedience, therefore, and all covenantal disobedience merits divine punishment. As Ponet warns, if subjects submitted to "idolaters and wicked livers, as the papists," then God will punish them with famine, pestilence, seditions, and wars.[83]

In the same vein, Goodman warns that failure to remove all idolatrous and tyrannical rulers would bring "the great wrath of God's indignation."[84] Failure to resist and remove is to conspire with princes, nobility, and evil people, according to Knox. God's

---

81. Christopher Goodman, *Superior Powers* (1958), cited in Edmund S. Morgan, *Puritan Political Ideas, 1558-1794* (Indianapolis, 1965), pp. 4, 5, 11 and Carlos M.N. Eire, *War Against the Idols—The Reformation of Worship from Erasmus to Calvin* (Cambridge: Cambridge University Press, 1986), p. 302.

82. Christopher Goodman, *Superior Powers* (Geneva, 1558), p. 180; John Knox, "The Appellation from the Sentence Pronounced by the Bishops and Clergy," in Laing (ed.), *The Complete Works of the John Knox*, vol. 4, p. 505; Carlos M.N. Eire, *War Against the Idols—The Reformation of Worship from Erasmus to Calvin* (Cambridge: Cambridge University Press, 1986), p. 302-3.

83. John Ponet, "A Short Treatise of Politicke Power," reprinted in W. S. Hudson, *John Ponet, Advocate of Limited Monarchy* (Chicago, 1942), pp. 176, 178.

84. Goodman, *Superior Powers* (1558), pp. 11, 93.

vengeance will punish the whole nation, the governors and the governed, for "conspiring together against Him and His holy ordinances."[85] Anything less than open rebellion, therefore, in the opinion of Ponet, Knox, and Goodman constitutes submission. Submission is conspiracy, conspiracy sin, and sin a guarantee of divine punishment.[86]

Knox's Own Summary of His Political Theology

In December 1577, the entire Scottish nobility signed a solemn covenant designating themselves the "congregation of Christ" bound to oppose the "congregation of Satan." Thus, according to Knox's thinking, "the people assembled together in one body of a Commonwealth, unto whom God has given sufficient force, not only to resist, but also to suppress all kind of open idolatry."[87]

John Knox addresses the Scottish nobility in his Appellation to the Nobility, his words a summary of his theology:

> I have offered unto you what God requireth of you, being placed above his people as rulers and princes; I have offered unto you and to the inhabitants of the realm the verity of Christ Jesus; and with the hazard of my life I presently offer to prove the religion which amongst you is maintained by fire and sword to be false, damnable, and diabolical. Which things if ye refuse, defending tyrants in their tyrrany, then dare I not flatter; but as it was commanded to Ezekiel boldly to proclaim, so must I cry to you that "you shall perish in your iniquity," that the Lord Jesus shall refuse so many of you as maliciously withstand his eternal verity, and in the days of his apparition, when all flesh shall appear before him, that he shall repel you from his company and shall command you to the fire which never shall be quenched; and then neither

---

85. Knox, "Appellation," *Works*, vol. 4, p. 498.

86. Carlos M.N. Eire, *War Against the Idols—The Reformation of Worship from Erasmus to Calvin* (Cambridge: Cambridge University Press, 1986), p. 303.

87. Knox's *History*, vol. 2, p. 122.

shall the multitude be able to resist neither yet the counsels of man be able to prevail against that sentence which he shall pronounce.[88]

Knox represents the most extreme application of magisterial Reformation political theology—believers have not only the right but the responsibility to rebel against "idolatrous" rulers.

CONCLUSION

The legal and political consensus of the Reformation is that error has no rights. Since the Bible is without error in the Reformation view, the Bible must govern law and politics—both political structure and political participants. Believing that each individual, because of original sin, has a depraved heart, being capable of tyranny, Reformers argued no one should have absolute power. The Bible and tyrants are perpetually in ideological war.

---

88. John Knox, *The Political Writings of John Knox—The First Blast of the Trumpet against the Monstrous Regiment of Women and Other Selected Works* (Washington: Folger Books, 1985), p. 144; for a concise biographies of the life of John Knox, see Ian Murray, *John Knox* (Carlisle, Pa.: Banner of Truth Trust, 1973); for a concise bibliography of John Calvin, see T.H.L. Parker, *John Calvin: A Biography*; perhaps the two best biographies of Calvin, see Alister E. McGrath, *A Life of John Calvin* (Oxford, 1990) and Ronald S. Wallace, *Calvin, Geneva, and the Reformation* (Edinburgh, 1989).

CONCLUSION

Although Calvin's worldview may appear distant to the modern legal and political theorist, a variety of maxims are profitable for consideration. First, Calvin believed that the highest form of government, deriving from biblical exegesis, was a constitutional republic. Calvin never governed Geneva; law governed Geneva. Calvin never unilaterally determined law; rather, he exegeted the Bible and argued his theories before the Consistory, composed of other ministers with whom he was an equal. The Consistory set policy, not Calvin. Elected representatives by the people, of the people, and for the people made law.

Second, Geneva was transformed from an ecclesiocratic feudal fiefdom into a constitutional republic because of a religious consensus. The religious consensus yielded a social, legal, and political consensus that made the constitutional republic work. Representative democracies do not work unless those who compose them want them to work. The American constitution, for instance, is not the force that makes America a republic; rather, the American constitution works because the American people voluntarily submit to it.

Third, church and state should not interrelate as co-belligerents, as if the gain of one is the loss of the other. The Genevan scheme allowed these two branches of society to nurture each other. Cooperation for the common good, without violation of either institution's integrity, resulted in a stable society, almost crime free by our standards.

CALVIN'S MAGISTERIAL INFLUENCE EXTENDED THROUGH PURITANISM

An Overview of Puritan Jurisprudence

What is the origin of Puritanism? It was an interdenominational movement that continued the Calvinistic Reformation of Christianity throughout the United Kingdom, and later in British Crown colonies. As early as John Jewell and Thomas Cartwright, Calvinistic reformers in the late sixteenth century were seen by their contemporaries as Puritan luminaries. Others of the seventeenth century included Stephen Charnock, Thomas Goodwin, John Owen, Thomas Boston, and Thomas Manton. These Puritans sought an intellectual, moral, and spiritual cleansing of the Church. Their standard of purity was the Bible, that is, the Old and New Testaments solely (Catholicism included the Apocrypha). The Westminster Confession of Faith, written by a symposium of 120 Puritan scholars from 1643 to 1648, expressed Puritan ideas in a comprehensive yet concise manner. Although this Confession formulated a Presbyterian form of church government, Separatist Puritans, Congregationalist Puritans, and Anglican Puritans alike embraced the theology forwarded by the Confession.[1] Cromwell's Protectorate of 1640–60 ended Puritan hegemony over British

---

1. Separatists sought to separate spheres of sovereignty, thus dividing state and church institutions; the Congregationalist, Presbyterian, and Anglican Puritans sought to establish state churches according to their own denominational distinctions.

CALVIN'S MAGISTERIAL INFLUENCE EXTENDED THROUGH PURITANISM

political, social, and ecclesiastical institutions. Jonathan Edwards, whose revivalist influence began in earnest in 1739, has been designated the last American Puritan; Puritan hegemony over Massachusetts society, however, ended around 1690, when a remnant of Puritan ideologues transferred from Massachusetts to Connecticut, resulting in the founding of Yale.

THE TELEOLOGY OF PURITAN JURISPRUDENCE

What were the objectives of Puritan jurisprudence? What kind of society did Puritan jurisprudence seek to build? Puritanism sought to produce a society where every individual, family, church, executive, legislature, and court submitted to law as laid down in the Bible. Their hope was for a universal theocracy. Under Puritan ideology, "the spirit of the whole creation was the reformation of the world."

> Reform in all places, all persons and callings. Reform the universities, reform the cities, reform the counties, reform inferior schools of learning, reform the Sabbath, reform the ordinances, the worship of God. Every plant which my heavenly father hath not planted shall be rooted up.[2]

Not only did the Puritans believe that they had received a divine mandate to build a universal theocracy, they believed that such a theocracy was prophesied in the Bible. In other words, they believed that since this kind of society would be established by God anyway; therefore, Puritans should cooperate with God to establish the Kingdom of heaven on earth, and since the same spiritual goals existed for each and every citizen, "progress toward that goal was thought to be a communal affair."[3] Puritan postmillennial

---

2. Sermon to the House of Commons, 1641, quoted in Rosenstock-Huessy, *Out of the Revolution: The Autobiography of Western Man* 291 (1938), in Harold J. Berman, "Religious Foundations of Law in the West: A Historical Perspective," *Journal of Law and Religion*, Volume 1, Number 1, Summer 1983, p. 30.

3. Jude P. Dougherty, "Puritan Aspiration, Puritan Legacy: An Historical/Philosophical Inquiry," *Journal of Law and Religion*, Volume 5, Number 1,

eschatology,[4] therefore, produced a social theory, and thus social theory guided the consequent jurisprudence.

The Vision of a National Puritan Utopia

The Puritan agenda for reform was interconnected, with key elements dedicated to the spiritual reformation of individuals, families, local assemblies, the national church at large, and the commonwealth.[5] An individual, according to Robert Bolton, had not achieved the Puritan vision until that individual walked with God. Bolton defined "walking with God" as a spiritual ideal:

> By walking with God, I mean, a sincere endeavour, punctually and precisely to manage, conduct, and dispose all our affairs, thoughts, words and deeds; all our behaviours, courses, carriage, and whole conversation, in reverence and fear, with humility and singleness of heart, as in the sight of an invisible God, under the perpetual presence of his all-seeing, glorious, pure eye; and by a comfortable consequent, to enjoy by the assistance and exercise of faith, an unutterable sweet communion, and humble familiarity with his holy majesty: In a word, to live in heaven upon earth.[6]

(1987), p. 113. Compare Thomas Hooker's analogy of the believers' departing from Babylon to journey toward Mount Zion. H.C. Porter, *Puritanism in Tudor England* (Columbia: University of South Carolina Press, 1971), p. 251.

4. The postmillennial system of eschatology holds that the kingdom of heaven will expand on earth until every nation becomes a Christian theocracy. After a period of universal prosperity (material and spiritual) under such a theocratic rule, Christ will return to establish a new heavens and new earth (*cf.* 2 Peter 3:10; Rev. 20:7-15). This was the dominant eschatology in the Puritan era, as evidenced by the consensus of Puritan scholars who produced the Westminster Confession of Faith, which included the Larger Catechism. The Larger Catechism's exposition of the Lord's Prayer, particularly the phrase, "thy kingdom come," delineates a postmillennial eschatology.

5. John H. Primus, *Holy Time—Moderate Puritanism and the Sabbath* (Macon, Georgia: Mercer University Press, 1989), p. 168.

6. Robert Bolton, *Some General Directions for a Comfortable Walking with God* (London, 1626), pp. 29-30.

Not only was the Puritan vision a spiritual metamorphosis of individuals, it included entire families, as Richard Greenham reminds us:

> And surely if men were careful to reform themselves first, and then their own families, they should see God's manifold blessings in our land upon Church and Commonwealth. For of particular persons come families; of families, towns; of towns, provinces; of provinces, whole realms: so that conveying God's holy truth in this sort from one to another, in time, and that shortly, it would so spread to all parts of this kingdom.[7]

The Puritan hope was nothing less than a total metamorphosis of the United Kingdom into a new Israel; furthermore, it was an Israel that would never fall either spiritually or otherwise. To create this society, its citizens were obliged to set aside a day for purposes of preaching and thoughtful reflection.

Sabbath Observance—The Crux of Puritan Social Theory

In order to initiate a spiritual metamorphosis within English society, Puritanism wanted to ascend a spiritual ladder that would take the country nearer to God. The foundation of Puritan social theory was strict Sabbatarianism, adherence to the fourth commandment. By a universal observance of the Sabbath for preaching and other spiritual exercises, they intended to amplify the effects of that preaching. John Ley referred to the Sabbath as "the training day of military discipline," observing it was "the sum and substance of all religion."[8] William Gouge held that one's entire personal sanctification depended upon observing it: "The very life of piety is preserved by a due sanctification of the Lord's day. They put a knife to the throat of religion, that hinder the same."[9]

---

7. Richard Greenham, *Works* (1599), p. 164.
8. John Ley, *Sunday a Sabbath* (London, 1641), sig. C4.
9. William Gouge, *The Whole Armour of God* (London, 1627), sig. A2.

Without Sabbath observance, Christians could not fulfill their spiritual potential. "Therefore we might learn to sanctify the Sabbath of the Lord, for else we shall never increase in faith, knowledge, or obedience as we should; for the begetting and increase whereof this day hath been set apart and sanctified from the beginning."[10] A common metaphor for the Sabbath was *marcatura animae*, or "the marketplace of the soul." Henry Burton amplified the metaphor: "Again, it is the market day of our souls, wherein we come to God's house the market place, to buy the wine and milk of the word, without money, or money worth. How is that? By hearing and heeding God's word, that truth whereby we are sanctified, John 17:17, and to pray unto him; thus by the word and prayer we are sanctified."[11] If observing the Sabbath waned, according to George Walker, so would decay all other spiritual exercises: "the most effectual ordinary means of grace and furtherances to eternal life and blessedness, would undoubtedly grow out of use, and at length utterly decay and vanish."[12] To Walker, the Sabbath was "the hedge of defense to true Christian religion." "Preaching, reading and hearing of the word . . . true piety, and the true knowledge and worship of God, and true faith in Christ, are upheld, maintained, increased and continued among all Christian nations from generation to generation."

To Cawdry and Palmer, the Sabbath was a weekly spiritual quintessence, a time when Christians reached their spiritual peak.[13] This zenith represented a victory in the invasion of the kingdom of God on earth. Heaven invaded earth, according to the Puritans' Deuteronomic vision, and without the Sabbath, this would not happen. Henry Burton explains:

---

10. William Perkins, *A Godly and Learned Exposition upon Revelation* (London, 1606), p. 45.

11. Henry Burton, *The Law and the Gospel Reconciled* (London, 1631), p. 64.

12. George Walker, *The Doctrine of the Sabbath* (Amsterdam, 1638), sig. A2.

13. Daniel Cawdry and Herbert Palmer, *The Christian Sabbath Vindicated* (London, 1645), Epistle to the reader.

so as from the right sanctification of the Lord's day doth spring all holiness, and power of religion, whereby God is honoured, the commonwealth itself is made glorious as being established and combined with the most firm bonds of pure religion, the crown and security of kings and kingdoms.[14]

Cawdry and Palmer saw England's spiritual and material prosperity linked to observing the Sabbath. Failure to do so explained why the English Reformation had failed, according to Cawdry and Palmer. "We think one main cause of these national judgments, under which this land now groans, was the public toleration of the profanation of the day."[15] The Puritan historian Primus interprets the "keeping of the Sabbath law" "as the key to all others."[16] Primus continues:

No wonder that, in their Deuteronomic vision, the welfare of the entire nation would stand or fall with the use or abuse of this holy time, with success or failure in performing the sacred duties of preparing for the Word, hearing the Word, reflecting upon the Word, and "doing" the Word. And no wonder that the appointment of such a critical time could not be left to the relatively untrustworthy discretion of sinful human institutions.[17]

John Sprint captures the expectancy, fervor, and strenuous nature of the phenomenon in his "Ode to the Sabbath."

A doctrine harmless, true, and holy, making thee holy and preparing thee to heaven, agreeing to the Scripture, to right reason, to common civility, and even to civil policies. A doctrine conforming us to the commandment of God, yea even to his blessed and holy image. A doctrine bringing much glory unto God, and benefit to man, knowledge to the ignorant, sense unto the hardened, direction to the willing, discipline to the

---

14. Burton, *Law and Gospel Reconciled*, p. 67.
15. Cawdry and Palmer, *The Christian Sabbath Vindicated*, sig. A2.
16. Primus, p. 180.
17. *Ibid.*

irregular, conscience to the obstinate, comfort to the conscienced, and bringing none inconvenience in the world. A doctrine that addeth face, fashion, growth and firmitude unto a church, strength and comely order to a commonwealth; giving propagation to the gospel, help and vigor to the laws; ease, honor, and obedience unto the governors; unity and quiet to the people; and lastly, certain happiness and blessing to them all. For the which doctrine whosoever argues, pleadeth for God, for his glory, for his worship, for his commandment and will, for his word, his sacraments, and invocation: for the law, for the gospel, for Moses, and the prophets, for Christ and his apostles, for the upholding and flourishing estate of the church and commonwealth, of schools and universities, and of the faithful ministry of Christ. In a word they plea for the wearied bodies rest, for the evil conscience quiet; for the sound practice of godliness and mercy, in a certain, settled, and constant order. And so by consequence for heaven itself.[18]

Either through responding to a parish sermon or observing law enacted in support of Sabbatarianism, the day was the center of Puritan social reformation.[19]

The Centrality of Preaching in Puritanism

Under Puritanism, "the real energy was supplied by the preacher."[20] "The essential thing in understanding the Puritans is that they were preachers before they were anything else."[21] "In the sermons preached from hundreds of Puritan pulpits . . . Puritan ideology was set forth in its totality."[22] Close personal ties united preachers,

18. John Sprint, *Propositions, Tending to Proove the Necessarie Use of the Christian Sabbaoth, or Lord's Day* (London: Thomas Man, 1607), pp. 35–36.

19. Primus, p. 168.

20. William Haller, *Rise of Puritanism* (New York: Columbia University Press, 1938), p. 15.

21. Irvonwy Morgan, *The Godly Preachers of the Elizabethan Church* (London: Epworth, 1965), p. 11.

22. Paul Seaver, *The Puritan Lectureships* (Stanford: Stanford University

CALVIN'S MAGISTERIAL INFLUENCE EXTENDED THROUGH PURITANISM

who called each other "brother."[23] The integrity and education of Puritan ministers were a welcomed contrast to other clergy of the period. "Duties neglected, nepotism, plurality, non-residence, self-indulgence, some immorality, and, above all, ignorance—these were characteristic of the Church and clergy."[24]

Only by preaching could clerical abuses and attendant degeneration be halted. No other spiritual exercise equaled the effects of preaching; even a sacrament, such as the Lord's Supper, was a meaningless ritual without the context of preaching.[25] Furthermore, reading the Scriptures without interpretative comment was scorned as a "dumb reading." During the English Reformation, the features of a true church were three: a faithful preaching of the Word, a faithful administration of the sacraments (the Lord's Supper and baptism), and Church discipline. William Whitaker in 1599 went a step further and reduced these to preaching alone.[26]

John More declaimed in Jeremiads a divine judgment against civil rulers if they forbad preachers from parish pulpits. "Unless there be preaching, the people perish: unless they have believed, they are damned, and believe can they not without preaching."[27] Lancelot Andrewes claimed that there could be no political justice without "prophetia,"[28] or "the careful looking to prophecy." Andrewes saw moral declension as the basic cause of the fall of great

---

Press, 1970), p. 5.

23. Actually, the appellation "brethren" connoted Puritanism in their day as much the appellation "comrade" connotes Communism in the present day. Irvonwy Morgan, *Prince Charles's Puritan Chaplain* (Ruskin House: George Allen, 1957), p. 41.

24. Paul A. Welsby, *Lancelot Andrewes* (London: SPCK, 1958), p. 65.

25. John S. Coolidge, *The Pauline Renaissance in England* (London: Clarendon, 1970), p. 142. David Little, *Religion, Order, and Law* (Oxford: Blackwell, 1970), pp. 68–70. John Calvin, *Institutes of the Christian Religion* (Philadelphia: Westminster, 1973), 4:1:5, 4:3:1.

26. William Whitaker, *Praelectiones* (Cambridge, 1599), pp. 387ff.

27. John More, *Three Godly Sermons* (Cambridge, 1594), introduction.

28. The Greek term *prophetia* includes both foretelling and forthtelling. The term encompasses the supernatural apprehension of the future and communication of future events, as well as simple communication of biblical and spiritual concepts.

nations; if a nation attended to the pure preaching of the Word, the nation would retain its political integrity. He illustrated this using a military metaphor. If the enemies of the United Kingdom sought to invade the island, where would they do so? Andrewes believed they would chosse the locales "where people are least taught the fear of God."[29]

Andrewes also decried the practice of allowing incompetents to preach:

> Since the dumb-dogs were lately beaten, every dunce took upon him to usurp the pulpit, where talking by the hour glass, and throwing forth headlong their incoherence, they have the luck forsooth to have it called by the name of preaching. The very Church is infested with as many fooleries of discourse as are commonly in the places where they shear sheep.

Of course, the Puritans favored laws that would force society to listen to their preaching; by such persuasion would their ministers saturate society with God's plan.

EXCURSUS—CONGREGATIONALIST PURITAN JURISPRUDENCE IN PRACTICE IN NEW ENGLAND

Substantive Puritan Law

Established by Pilgrims in 1620 and Congregationalist Puritans in 1630, the Massachusetts Bay Colony was essentially a child of England's Congregationalist Puritan sect. The new colony trained its ministers at Cambridge, a center of Puritan thought and practice during this time. In the New World, enacting law was less at the mercy of the enemies created by the Puritan revolution. Unhampered by the factionalism that had occurred in England, the colony was a religious society that was structured around laws derived from the Bible. More than anywhere else, the Puritan concept of the reformation of the world provided a theory of law dedicated to

---

29. Lancelot Andrewes, *The Moral Law Expounded* (London, 1642), pp. 301ff.

religious reformation. The objective was to reform both state and church.

In England, during the 1640s and 1650s, over ten thousand pamphlets were published arguing for legal reforms.[30] The New England Puritans held:

> Whatsoever ordinance of the Old Testament is not repealed in the New Testament, as peculiar to the Jewish Paedagogie, but was of moral and perpetual equity, the same binds us in these days, and is to be accounted the revealed will of God in all ages, though it be not particularly and expressly mentioned in the writings of the New Testament . . . the Scriptures of the New Testament do speak little in these cases; only the Scripture of the Old Testament do give direction and light about them.[31]

The concept of Christian reformation complemented the political doctrine civil law, as we see from this extract (Massachusetts Body of Liberties of 1641):[32]

> 1. If any man after legal conviction shall have or worship any other God, but the Lord God, he shall be put to death.[33]
>
> 2. If any man or woman be a witch, (that is hath or consulteth with a familiar spirit), They shall be put to death.[34]

---

30. Berman, p. 30.

31. *An Apology of the Churches in New England for Church-Covenant* (London, 1643), p. 8, as quoted by John F. Wilson, *Pulpit in Parliament* (Princeton: University Press, 1969), p. 143.

32. Berman, p. 30.

33. Exodus 20:1-6; Deuteronomy 5:6-10; Both of the previous texts are the narrative record given at Mt. Sinai in Exodus 19. The order of the commandments is significant. The Massachusetts Bay Colony began its basic code of law the same way that the Israelite nation of long ago began theirs—worship of the God of the Bible was the only worship. This canon is in keeping with Exodus 22:20, "he that sacrificeth unto any god, save unto the Lord only, he shall be utterly destroyed."

34. Exodus 22:18: "Thou shalt not suffer a witch to live"; Deuteronomy 18:9-11: "There shalt not be found among you anyone who maketh his son or his daughter pass through the fire, or who useth divination, or an observer of times, or an enchanter, or a witch, or a charmer, or a consulter of mediums,

3. If any man shall Blaspheme the name of God, the Father, the Son or Holy Ghost, with direct, express, presumptuous or high handed blasphemy, or shall curse God in the like manner, he shall be put to death.[35]

4. If any person commit any willful murder, which is manslaughter, committed upon premeditated malice, hatred or Cruelty, not in a man's necessary just defense, nor be mere casually against his will, he shall be put to death.[36]

5. If any person slayeth another suddenly in his anger or Cruelty of passion, he shall be put to death.[37]

---

or a wizard, or a necromancer. For all these things are an abomination unto the Lord."

35. Essentially, this third canon in the law of Massachusetts Bay is a particularization of the first. The first canon prohibited worship of any other god; this canon focuses on any evil speaking against the God of the Bible. This canon is an application of Exodus 20:1–6 and Deuteronomy 5:6–10.

Speaking against God was so abominable to the Puritans of Massachusetts Bay that they applied the death penalty. The Puritan application of the death penalty patterns the execution described in Leviticus 24:1–16, 23. Leviticus 24:10–16 records the first implementation of this commandment. In this narrative, "the son of an Israelitish woman" blasphemed the Hebrew God Yahweh. Moses commanded that the party be put in custody until he could inquire of the Yahweh what should be done. Yahweh's verdict was "he who blasphemeth the name of the Lord, he shall surely be put to death" (Leviticus 24:16). In Leviticus 24:23 this judgment was executed against the blasphemer.

36. Genesis 9:6, "Whoso sheddeth man's blood, by man shall his blood be shed." In Exodus 20:13, Moses issues the command prohibiting murder, "Thou shalt not kill." The Hebrew term *hag* may mean any form of killing. However, the term is interpreted in Exodus 21:23, where Moses orders that "thou shalt give life for life." The Mosaic *lex talionis* required that anyone who took another's life must lose their own. The Exodus 20:13 injunction against murder is repeated in Deuteronomy 5:17.

37. This fifth canon particularizes the fourth. It focuses the colonists' attention upon what we would describe as manslaughter today. The Puritans placed colonists on notice they would not tolerate the violent expression of emotion. Regarding manslaughter, the Puritans applied Exodus 20:13 and 21:23, thus eliminating an entire category of law. To them, capital punishment was an unambiguous response to murder, whatever its origins.

6. If any person shall slay another through guile, either by poisoning or other such devilish practice, he shall be put to death.[38]

7. If any man or woman shall lie with any beast or brute creature by Carnal Copulation, They shall surely be put to death. And the beast shall be slain and buried and not eaten.[39]

8. If any man lieth with mankind as he lieth with a woman, both of them have committed abomination, they both shall surely be put to death.[40]

9. If any person committeth Adultery with a married or espoused wife, the Adulterer and Adulteress shall surely be put to death.[41]

10. If any man stealeth a man or mankind, he shall surely be put to death.[42]

---

38. This is yet another particularization regarding murder. Whereas in the previous canon, manslaughter was the focus, the sixth turns on two forms of murder: deception and poisoning. Again, the Body of Liberties applied Exodus 20:13 and 21:23.

39. Exodus 22:19 states "Whosoever lieth with a beast shall surely be put to death." The Puritans extended judicial remedies even to animals, indicating hatred of sexual deviation.

40. Deuteronomy 27:20–23 specifies which sexual practices are forbidden. The Puritans applied this, as well as Leviticus 18, proscribing sexual behavior for themselves. These passages forbid marriage with parents-in-law and siblings-in-law. Further, the death penalty applies to homosexuality.

41. Exodus 20:14 is the general moral command against adultery (Deuteronomy 5:18). A New Testament passage, John 8:1–12, poses a seeming contradiction. Yet in John 8, Christ commanded a woman taken in adultery, "Go and sin no more." If Christ obeyed biblical law, why would he pardon the woman at the well? One possible resolution of the apparent discrepancy is that Christ acted as a priest in this passage. Priests were to have compassion on those who had fallen out of God's way. Christ functioned as a priest, as distinguished from his role as a king.

42. Exodus 21:16 states that "he that stealeth a man, and selleth him, or if he be found in his hand, he shall surely be put to death."

11. If any man rise up by false witness, wittingly and of purpose to take away any man's life, he shall be put to death.[43]

12. If any man shall conspire and attempt any invasion, insurrection, or public rebellion against our commonwealth, or shall indeavour to surprise any town or Towns, fort or forts therein, or shall treacherously and perfidiously attempt the alteration and subversion of our fame or politics or Government fundamentals he shall be put to death.[44]

This code reflects a Calvinistic schema for determining the relation between church and state, for to the Calvinist, God was king, reigning over both church and state. The magistrate's Address, the General Law of New Plymouth in 1658, states "God being a God of order and not of confusion hath commanded in his word and put man into a capacity in some measure to observe and be guided by good and wholesome laws."[45] Just as the church is regulated by a divine Sovereign, so the state must be regulated also. Puritans called these dictates "liberties," a term that strikes us as ironic today, in these more liberal times. To the Puritans, laws that accorded with the Bible freed them from evil. To the Puritans, the terms law and liberty were synonymous.

The Cohesive Social Order Established by Puritan Law

When the Puritans erected their "city upon a hill" in 1629, they established a political texture different from that of other colonies.

---

43. The Puritans regarded Exodus 20:13 and 21:23 as inviolable; they applied the death penalty to anyone who would perjure themselves in death penalty cases. If false testimony caused the death of anyone, the party responsible would receive the same sentence.

44. *Colonial Laws of Massachusetts,* compiled by Order of the City Council of Boston, in Charles Dunn, *American Political Theology, Historical Perspective and Theoretical Analysis* (New York: Praeger Publishers, 1984), pp. 22–23.

45. The Address to the General Laws of New Plymouth (1698), 11 Records of the Colony of New Plymouth Laws, 1623–1682, (Pulsifer, ed. 1861), cited by Berman, p. 30.

Conflicting groups from New York and Pennsylvania vied in the political and economic arena.[46] Meanwhile, the southern royalist colonies endured class violence and a fight for survival; furthermore, their fear of a growing black population alarmed the white aristocracy.[47] In the Bay Colony, however, social unrest was rare; rather, Massachusetts was remarkably cohesive. Differences revolved around religious issues such as the Half-Way Covenant, and policy concerns, such as regulating navigation to appease the Crown.[48] In fact, it was the biblical laws that provided a social amalgum, since their severity inspired vigilance. Since the law informed the Massachusetts school system as well, the society developed commonality that bound citizens together. Unlike Pennsylvania, where the Dutch Reformed taught children in Dutch and Quakers taught according to their creed (Swedish Covenant churches also taught their children according to creed and language), only a small minority of the Massachusetts colonists were not Puritan, and all spoke English. This commonality, of creed and language, was unique to the Massachusetts colony.[49]

A Portait of a Victim of Puritan Jurisprudence: Obadiah Holmes

It was Obadiah Holmes' misfortune to be a Baptist in a rigidly Puritan Colony, since in 1644 the General Court of the colony had passed a statute against Baptists. The preamble of this resolution includes the following:

> For as much as experience hath plentifully and often proved that, since the first rising of the Anabaptists, about one hundred years since, these have been incendiaries

---

46. William Pencak, *War, Politics, and Revolution in Provincial Massachusetts* (Boston: Northeastern University Press, 1981), p. 2.

47. *Ibid.*

48. William Pencak, *War, Politics, and Revolution in Provincial Massachusetts* (Boston: Northeastern University Press, 1981), pp. 2–6.

49. Thomas Jefferson Wertenbaker, *The Puritan Oligarchy—The Founding of American Civilization* (New York: Charles Scriber's Sons, 1947).

of commonwealths and infectors of persons in the main matter of religion and troublers of churches in all places where they have been.

This indictment of all branches of Anabaptist faith reflected an American Puritan consensus. In conclusion the statute says:

> It is ordered and decreed that if any person or persons within this jurisdiction either openly condemn or oppose the baptizing of infants or shall deny the ordinance of magistracy or their lawful right to punish the outward breaches of the First Table every such person or persons shall be banished from the colony.

In 1649 Obadiah Holmes and other Baptists who worshipped under the Rev. Samuel Newman withdrew and established their own church at Swansea, a town Holmes and his followers named after a small city in Wales.[50] In the year 1651 three Baptists (Clark, the founder and pastor of the Baptist congregation in Newport, Crandall, and Obadiah Holmes) were seized by authorities when the men visited Lynn. The three were accused of propaganda. Crandal and Clark received heavy fines only, but Holmes was imprisoned and later publicly flogged.[51] (A more zealous activist by the name of Endecott advocated the execution of Clark, Crandall, and Holmes.) Holmes complained to Oliver Cromwell, since one of Holmes' associates, a Mr. Leveret, had been a captain of calvary under Cromwell, and Holmes and Leveret thought that Leveret could obtain a favor from Cromwell. The hope vanished when Cromwell responded that "the evil seducers" ought to be banished from the colony.[52]

In general, authorities became increasingly intolerant of divergent opinion. In 1646 Cromwell's Lord's Protectorate passed a law requiring that all heretics "continuing obstinate therein, after due means of conviction, shall be sentenced to banishment." In

50. Albert Bushnell Hart, *A Commonwealth History of Massachusetts* (New York: The States History Company, 1927), I:528–29.

51. Hart, I:481.

52. Thomas Hutchinson, *The History of the Colony and Province of Massachusetts Bay* (Cambridge: Harvard University Press, 1936), I:164–65.

CALVIN'S MAGISTERIAL INFLUENCE EXTENDED THROUGH PURITANISM

1651, when the Cambridge Platform was drafted by the clergy and magistrates, a provision included that "the magistrate is to put forth his coercive power, as the matter shall require" in cases of discipline for heresy.[53] In 1658, the Declaration of Liberties was amended so that no one in the colony who attended a church "which shall be gathered without the approbation of the magistrates and the said churches, shall be admitted to the freedom of this commonwealth.[54] The Puritans therefore, denied freedom to any who did not acknowledge their laws.

THE RELATION OF PURITAN COVENANT THEOLOGY AND THE PURITAN SOCIOLOGY

The Puritan social contract was a religious version of Rousseau's. Rousseau saw this as a meeting of the minds, where those comprising a state decreed the nature of their social order. Rousseau believed the social contract derived from mutual assent between citizens, and that God was not a party to this. To the Puritan, however, God was the initiator and administrator of a binding contract between himself and humankind. The core of the Puritan society was the interconnection between God and all citizens, in order to form a heavenly contract, which consisted of the mutual assent of divine and human participants.[55]

In 1641 the Puritan George Walker wrote that the "word covenant in our English tongue signifies, as we all know, a mutual promise, bargain, and obligation between two parties." Although Walker confines the parties of a covenant to two, his thinking was actually broader. He saw every contract between two individuals as actually a contract between three individuals, the two parties and God.[56] God was part of their daily commerce, as historian Zaret

53. Hart, I:82.

54. Hart, I:481.

55. David Zaret, *The Heavenly Contract—Ideology and Organization in Pre-Revolutionary Puritanism* (Chicago: The University of Chicago Press, 1985), pp. 130–136.

56. George Walker, *The Manifold Wisdom of God* (1641), pp. 39, 40 cited

observes: "... in the form of a heavenly contractor, God became less remote and unknowable. No longer was God unaccountable for God condescended to use a human device, a contract, in his dealings with humanity."[57] Another Puritan, Richard Sibbes, expands on this:

> All the gracious promises of the Gospel are not only promises upon condition, and so a covenant, but likewise the covenant of grace is a testament and a will (a will is made without conditions; a covenant with conditions), that as he has made a covenant what he would have us to do, so his testament is that we shall have the grace to do so.[58]

The concept of a heavenly contract produced a vigilant, active group conscience. Puritans knew that unless they kept the conditions of the heavenly contract, God would repay[59]; if they observed the contract, God would reward. Not only was covenant theology a social ethic that controlled society through laws, but also worked from within, by activating a distinctly Puritan conscience.

THE INFLUENCE OF THE PURITAN WAR WITH CHARLES AND THE PRELATES ON PURITAN LEGAL THEORY

"The first casualty of war is truth," so says the adage, one that those loyal to King Charles leveled at Puritan lawyers and ministers who by their sermons to Parliament became its legal ideologues and social policymakers. The Puritan revolution entailed a violent clash of worldviews. What began as an effort to free the pulpits from the Papacy and other manifestations of Rome developed into war to destroy the prelacy and monarchy both. One side was

---

by Zaret, p. 169.

57. Zaret, pp. 167–68.

58. Richard Sibbes, *Christ's Exaltation Purchast by Humiliation*, in *The Works of Richard Sibbes* (1639), 5, 342, as quoted by Zaret, p. 169.

59. Zaret, p. 169.

the status quo—represented by the monarchy and the prelacy. When King James I was confronted with Millenary Petition in 1608, where 1000 Presbyterian Puritans signed a petition for an English Presbyterian church, the King shouted "I will harry them out of the land." To James, who was supreme head of the Anglican state church (thanks to Elizabeth's Act of Supremacy), "no bishop" meant "no king." On the other side, the Puritans, by whatever means necessary, sought to replace a corrupted system of authority with a new authority structure built around a Calvinistic model of the church-state. Each side claimed to be "champions of law."[60] Each side accused the other of "setting themselves above law and usurping the sovereignty of the state."[61] Although King Charles I blamed the disaffection of his subjects most of all upon Puritan preachers, Puritan lawyers came to evoke public opinion just as vigorously, particularly at commencement of hostilities in March 1642.[62] The break between Charles and Parliament resulted in a plethora of Puritan declarations, manifestos, and pamphlets on law and religion,[63] including a pamphlet that called into question the presumptions of divine right:

> A question answered: How Laws[64] are to be understood, and obedience yielded. The answer was that there is in Laws an equitable, and literal sense. Command of the militia may be entrusted by law to the king for the public good to serve which is the reason and equity of law. But when any commander whatever acts contrary to the public good, then he himself gives liberty to the Commanded to refuse *obedience* to the Letter. Not need this *equity* be expressed in the Law, being so naturally implied and supposed in all Laws. Parliament cannot be required to vote its own destruction. A general may

---

60. William Haller, *Liberty and Reformation in the Puritan Revolution* (New York: Columbia University Press, 1955), p. 72.

61. Haller, p. 72.

62. Haller, pp. 71, 73.

63. Haller, p. 73.

64. Capitalization, italics, and spelling are true to the original in this quotation.

not turn his guns on his own men. Were he to do so, he would *ipso facto* estate them in a right of disobedience, except we think that obedience binds Men to cut their own throats.⁶⁵

The reference to suicide is seminal to Puritan thinking. If the King, who ruled by divine right, ordered a subordinate to cut his own throat, even the ignorant would conclude that the command cannot emanate from God because suicide, as self-murder, violates the sixth commandment. The Puritan worldview presupposes a higher law than man's; through understanding the Bible and their own consciences, subjects are acquainted with higher law. To Puritans, law was all-powerful. They believed that as God gave the law to Moses to govern Israel, and God gave nations his law in the Bible as well, this law took precedence over kings and subjects alike. Not only had Christians the right but the responsibility to obey God's law rather than man's, if they contradicted each other.⁶⁶ If a monarch ruled, this was the tyranny of monarchy; if a group ruled, this was the tyranny of oligarchy; if the majority ruled, this was tyranny of the majority. When God ruled, however, to the Puritan mind this was liberty.

Prior to the revolution, the doctrine of higher law had found a powerful exposition in Christopher St. Germain's *Dialogue in English, betweene a Doctor of Divinitie, and a Student in the Lawes of England*, (commonly referred to as *The Doctor and the Student*). St. Germain's work held the greatest sway upon the lawyers and

---

65. *A Question Answered*, dated April 21, 1642, as quoted by Haller, p. 73.

66. In this respect the Puritans surpassed their theological mentor, John Calvin. Calvin held that it was the right of Christians to rebel against a religiously oppressive governments but not their responsibility. Calvin's view of the right of Christians to rebel is qualified however; only the Christian magistrate, as a representative of Christian subjects, had the right to resist tyranny. "To withstand the fierce licentiousness of kings," Calvin wrote, lower magistrates, as protectors of the community under them, are to have the divine right and duty of constitutional resistance to tyranny. John Knox, Calvin's pupil, was one of the second-generation reformers who moved a step beyond Calvin. Knox believed it was not only the option but the duty of Christians to rebel against a government that did not submit to the higher law. John Calvin, *Institutes of the Christian Religion* (Phil.: Westminster Press, 1973), IV:20, pp. 1518–1519.

CALVIN'S MAGISTERIAL INFLUENCE EXTENDED THROUGH PURITANISM

lawmakers of the Puritan era. The overarching idea that circumscribed his works was that courts of equity, by setting up rules of equity based upon the Bible, universal reason, and conscience, could "supply inadequacies and correct injustices arising under the laws of states."[67] St. German taught English lawyers that God "imprinted the law of nature in every man, teaching him what is it be done, and what is to be fled. This law must be obeyed upon peril of one's soul, and it cannot be contravened by human custom, enactment, or decree."[68] Accordingly, the English common lawyer John Lilburne, a Member of Parliament throughout the 1640s, would enter the House of Commons with his Bible in one hand and the *Institutes* in the other.[69] Parliament seized upon this doctrine in order to justify its crusade against Charles I. Parliament, and those who supported it, saw this governing body as the embodiment of divinely given law, supervening the corrupted rule of monarchy.

THE PURITAN IDEOLOGY OF CHURCH AND STATE

In Cambridge of the late sixteenth century, a Puritan luminary emerged who pioneered the distinctives of the Presbyterian branch of English Puritanism regarding the roles of church and state. Thomas Cartwright's view of these is derived from Calvin's *Institutes*, the most widely read theology of both the sixteenth and seventeenth centuries.[70] Cartwright defines the distinction between

67. Haller, p. 72.
68. Haller, p. 72.
69. Berman, p. 33.

70. "No other theological work was so widely read and so influential from the Reformation to the American Revolution. At least seventy-four editions in nine languages, besides fourteen abridgments, appeared before the Puritan exodus to America, an average edition annually for three generations." In 1578, the *Institutes* and Calvin's Catechism was required of all Oxford undergraduates. Until Archbishop Laud's supremacy in the 1630s, the *Institutes* was the key theological treatise in England among Anglicans and the various Puritan sects. Even Laud spoke subdued praise for the *Institutes*: the *Institutes* "may profitably be read as one of their first books of divinity." But Laud cautioned

church and state, the interrelation of church and state, and the function of ecclesiastical governments and political government.

Cartwright's Teaching of the Distinction of the Church and State

The historical origins of the English Puritan movement were predicated on the eclipse of the church. Beginning with Henry the Eighth's reign, the monarch of England was also the head of the English state church, according to the Act of Supremacy; hence all political, legal, and ecclesiastical activities were under the auspices of the Crown. This eclipse of church sovereignty by the state prompted one late sixteenth-century theologian, Whitgift, to state:

> If the church and commonwealth were under a Christian Prince all one:[71] it should follow, that whosoever is a part of one, should needs be a part of the other: and contrawise, whosoever is cut of from one, must be cut of from the other.[72]

Whitgift's unified view of church and state inspired Thomas Cartwright of Cambridge to respond according to the Calvinist "two kingdoms" doctrine.[73] Although Cartwright views both

---

against New College students from reading it "so soon." "I am afraid it... doth too much possess their judgment... and makes many of them humorous in, if not against the church." Herbert D. Foster, *Collected Papers* 78 (privately printed, 1929), as quoted by Berman, p. 25.

71. Spelling in this quotation is true to the sixteenth-century original.

72. A.F. Scott Pearson, *Church and State—Political Aspects of Sixteenth Century Puritanism* (Cambridge: At the University Press, 1927), p. 10. Note that Cartwright's works have been out of print since the 19th century; therefore, all quotes issue from Pearson's work, *Church and State*.

73. The Roman Catholic doctrine of the "two swords" evolved, under the Calvinistic phase of the Protestant reformation, into the "two kingdoms." The phrase "two swords" first appeared in a letter from Pope Gelasius I to Emperor Anastasius in the late 400s, where the Pope held that the imperial sphere of social order and lawmaking belonged to the Emperor and the spiritual sphere of spirituality belonged to the Pope. Boniface VIII, however, in 1302 ascribed both spheres to be ruled by the Pope, who wielded both secular or temporal and ecclesiastical or spiritual swords. Bearman, p. 15. Calvin taught the theory

church and state as thoroughly religious entities, he did not view them as one. Cartwright proposes that the "church and state should be two self-sufficient complete and distinct, but related societies."[74] Cartwright defends his thesis by texts from the Old Testament, using the words of Christ, the Apostolic Church, and post-Apostolic church fathers. According to Cartwright's interpretation, the Judaean King Jehoshaphat set a normative example of church-state relations in 2 Chronicles 19:11, appointing separate functionaries over ecclesiastical and governmental duties. Some officials were given authority over "all matters of the Lord," others over "all the king's matters."[75] According to Cartwright, 2 Chronicles 19:11 forbad an individual from holding an ecclesiastical and political office simultaneously. Earlier, John Jewel argued that an individual could hold ecclesiastical and political office simultaneously. Jewell points out that Samuel, although a prophet *to* Israel, was also a judge *over* Israel. To this example (including other Old Testament prophets who were rulers also, including Abraham, David, and Solomon), Cartwright responds:

> Some sharper Adversary[76] might here have objected: that Moses, David, and Solomon, being princes in the most flourishing estate of the church: did notwithstanding make church orders. Whereunto I answer, that they did so, partly, for that they were not kings only and princes, but also prophets of God: partly, for that they had special and express direction thereto from God by the prophets: whereby they did even those things in the church, which, without such special revelation, was not lawful for the priests themselves to have done.

of the two kingdoms, but the church and state were each severally responsible to God. After Cartwright, the Scottish Presbyterian Puritan Samuel Rutherford wrote *Lex Rex*, where he appealed to the law of nature written upon the hearts of all mankind, the ultimate sovereignty of the people, the origin of government in a covenant between God, the governor, and the governed, and the right of resistance when that covenant was broken. Later, John Locke would coin the Calvinistic political arguments in the late 1680s and 1690s.

74. Pearson, p. 10.
75. Pearson, p. 11.
76. Spelling, punctuation, and capitalization are true to the original.

> And although the truth of this answer be apparent: yet, that it may have the more authority, especially with the D[octor] that tasteth nothing without this sauce; he may understand that it is M. Calvins answer of Moses, and that in this present cause now debated.[77]

Cartwright's view of overlapping ecclesiastical and political powers (Moses, David, and Solomon for example) makes distinction between "extraordinary" and "ordinary" offices in Scripture. The former were filled by those endowed with a supernatural ability, with a knowledge of the future, and the power to perform miracles. On the other hand, ordinary officers included those who, like the Levitical priests, fulfilled their duties ordinarily, that is, devoid of any supernatural knowledge or ability. Citing quotations from Christ, Cartwright argues that church and state were distinct entities. Christ's example, according to Cartwright, defines the distinction: "our Savior Christ, having the spirit without measure, refused as a thing unmete for his minstery, the office of a Judge."[78] In defense, Cartwright quotes Luke 12:13, "Master, bid my brother divide the inheritance with me." Christ responds, "man who made me a judge or a divider over you?" Cartwright deduces from this that ecclesiastical officials should not meddle in matters of civil authority.[79] Using Matthew 20:25, Mark 10:42, and Luke 22:25, Cartwright cites Christ's admonition to the sons of Zebedee's wife that they should not exercise dominion as the princes of Gentiles do, but seek to be the servant of all.[80] When Christ refuses to administer a civil judgment in the case of a woman taken in adultery (John 8:1–12), Cartwright deduces that the refusal was tantamount to a separation of ecclesiastical from judicial authority. Moses would have put the woman to death because he was supreme judge of the fledgling state of Israel in 1446 B.C.; Christ forgave the woman because he was head of a spiritual and ecclesiastical entity, the Christian church of A.D. 30. Cartwright also argues using the Apostles

---

77. Pearson, p. 12.
78. Pearson, p. 10.
79. Pearson, p. 10.
80. Pearson, p. 11.

as his example, that church and state are distinct entities in the biblical sense. He draws a dubious analogy on this point, however. Since elders are endowed with spiritual gifts, but earthly matters were relegated to deacons, so ecclesiastical matters belonged to the church and civil matters to the state. In speaking against "mingling of civil and ecclesiastical estates," Cartwright mentions the post-apostolic father Ambrose, who would not allow doctrinal issues to be deliberated in civil courts. Cartwright further identifies his position as opposite to that of Augustine, differing also with his own contemporaries, the reformers Calvin, Beza, and Bucer.[81] In sum, Cartwright argues that a minister should not concurrently serve as a judge, because the ministerial function:

> Is of greater weight then the strongest back can bear, of wider compass then the largest handes can faddam: a soldiarfare that will be only attended upon: seeing also it tendeth to the destruction of the body when one member encroacheth upon the office of another: and the civil Magistrate may by the same right invade the office of the Minister as he the office of the civil Magistrate.[82]

Cartwright's Teaching on the Relation Between Church and State

Cartwright's analysis of the relationship between church and state argues the church's superiority. The state is healthy only while the church is healthy: "the church is the foundation of the world, and therefore the common wealth builded upon it . . ."[83] In 1647, another Puritan, Samuel Richardson, framed the issue of which should dominate the other: "either the civil, or the spiritual state must be supreme: which of these must judge the other in spiritual matters?" To Richardson, the ecclesiastical realm takes precedence

---

81. Pearson, pp. 13–14.

82. Pearson, p. 14.

83. Pearson, p. 17.

over the political.⁸⁴ Similarly, Cartwright sees the primacy of the church over society:

> As the house is before the hangings and therefore the hangings which come after must be framed to the house which was before, so the church being before there was any commonwealth, and the commonwealth coming after must be fashioned and made suitable unto the church. Otherwise God is made to give place to men, heaven to earth.⁸⁵

Cartwright calls on magistrates to "submit their scepters, to throw down their crowns before the church,"⁸⁶ believing that the state exists to provide an orderly and efficient environment for the church to fulfill her mandate by gathering the "full number of the elect."⁸⁷ Cartwright analogizes the relation of church and state through allusion to the mythological twins of Hippocrates. When one twin laughs, the other laughs; when one weeps, the other weeps,⁸⁸ meaning that when the church is negligent, her negligence results in some cognizable wound in the state, or as Pearson states his summary of Cartwright's view: "deficiencies of the one produce deficiencies in the other. The commonwealth will not flourish until the church is reformed."⁸⁹ Cartwright's analogy of the Hippocrates twins implies that church and state are symbiotically bound together. The church depends upon the state to

---

84. Samuel Richardson, *The Necessity of Toleration in Matters of Religion*. *King's Pamphlets*, E. 407 (18), p. 11, as quoted by G.B. Tatham, *The Puritans in Power—A Study in the History of the English Church from 1640 to 1660* (Cambridge: At the University Press, 1913), p. 215.

85. Pearson, pp. 16–17. For too long Puritan ministers were limited by the civil laws of Anglican-controlled offices. For examples of how Puritan ministers circumvented these restrictions, see Ronald D. Marchant, *The Puritans and the Church Courts in the Diocese of York, 1560–1642* (Aberdeen: Longmans, 1960), pp. 83ff.

86. Margo Todd, *Christian Humanism and the Puritan Social Order* (Cambridge: Cambridge University Press, 1987), p. 195.

87. Pearson, p. 17.

88. Pearson, p. 19.

89. Pearson, p. 20.

provide an external social order, under which the church spreads the Gospel and even disciples its adherents. Cartwright compares the need of the church for the state to the need of all life for the sun.[90] The state needs the church, whose duty it is to change citizens from within, into governable, law-abiding, and contributing members of society. A commonwealth "without the church cannot long survive," Cartwright declaimed.[91] If the church's message (God's word) is "despised or abridged of a free and full course, princes, magistrates, and their commonwealths go to wreck or decay." "The want of the word of God produces a corresponding want of prosperity in the state."[92] Defending this view, Cartwright cites Proverbs 8:15 and Isaiah 60:12: "by me[93] kings reign, and princes decree justice"; "for nation and kingdom that will not serve thee shall perish." Cartwright (as quoted by Whitgift) furthers his argument by drawing on Proverbs 8:15 and Isaiah 60:12:

> It is true that we ought to be obedient unto the civil magistrate which governeth the church of God in that office which is committed unto him and according to that calling. But it must be remembered that civil magistrates must govern it according to the rules of God prescribed in his word, and that as they are nurses so they be servants unto the church, and as they rule in the church so they must remember to subject themselves unto the church, to submit their sceptres, to throw down their crowns, before the church, yea, as the prophet spaketh [Isaiah 49:23],[94] to lick the dust of the feet of the church. Wherein I mean not that the church doth either wring

90. *Ibid.*, p. 20.

91. *Ibid.*

92. Pearson, pp. 20–21.

93. Most Christian commentators of Proverbs 8 hold that the discourse's subject is Christ. This text would be interpreted "by Christ kings reign." In Cartwright's worldview, Christ can not be known except through his disciples who communicate the Word.

94. Isaiah 49:23: "And kings will be your guardians, and their princesses your nurses. They will bow down to you with their faces to the earth, and lick the dust of your feet; and you will know that I am the Lord; those who hopefully wait for me will not be put to shame."

the sceptre out of the princes' hands, to take their crowns from their heads, or that it requireth princes to lick the dust of her feet (as the pope under this pretense hath done), but I mean, as the prophet meaneth, that whatsoever magnificence, or excellency, or pomp, is either in them, or in their estates and commonwealths, which doth not agree with the simplicity and (in the judgment of the world) poor and contemptible estate of the church, that they will be content to lay down.[95]

Cartwright's conception of any government official, whether a hereditary monarch or elected, is that the official is chiefly a servant of God. Earthly rulers must obey the commands of God in the Scriptures.[96] (Were Cartwright alive today, some would call him a theonomist or Christian reconstructionist.)[97]

Cartwright's Teaching on the Nature of Church Government and State Government

Cartwright's most significant contribution to the Puritan movement is his exposition and apologetics for Presbyterian government, developed in lectures at Cambridge on the Book of Acts. His method is *ad fontes*, "return to the sources," that is, the books of the Bible.[98] His influence on Presbyterianism earned him recognition as the father of Presbyterian Puritanism. Cartwright believes that both the church and state are theocracies.[99] The government of the state and the government of the church are coterminous under

---

95. Pearson, p. 26 quoting the *Works of John Whitgift*, volume 3, p. 189.

96. Pearson, pp. 26–27.

97. For an overview of the theonomic or Christian reconstructionist framework, see Greg Bahnsen, *Theonomy in Christian Ethics* (Philipsburg: Craig Press, 1979).

98. William Furke, *Elizabethan Puritanism* (New York: Oxford University Press, 1971), p. 235.

99. He believed, however, that the Presbyterian church should be the church of the entire nation. C. E. Whiting, *Studies in English Puritanism from the Restoration to the Revolution* (New York: Augustus M. Kelley Publishers, 1968), p. 46.

one governor, who is God. The framework of the ecclesiastical government that Cartwright fashions from the Book of Acts was fundamentally anti-monarchy, his framework democratic and republican. It was democratic in that he believed that congregations should have a say in the determination of their ministers. Writing on the election of an assembly's ministers, Cartwright argued:

> Which things, if they have grounds in civil affairs, they have much better in ecclesiastical. For it is much more unreasonable that there should be thrust upon me a governor of whom the everlasting salvation or damnation both of my body and soul doth depend, than him of whom my wealth and commodity of this life doth hand; unless those upon whom he were thrust were fools, or madmen, or children, without all discretion of ordering themselves.[100]

It was up to congregations to vote for ministers who would represent them. Further, these elected ministers should meet in higher bodies called Presbyteries to vote on matters of church dogma and praxis. Similarly, Cartwright asserts that political sovereignty should depend on the consent of the governed:

> It is said among lawyers and indeed reason, which is the law of all nations, confirmeth it, *Quod omnium interest ab omnibus approbari debet:* 'That which standeth all men upon should be approved of all men. Which law hath this sense, that if it may be, it were good that those things which shall bind all men, and which require the obedience of all, should be concluded, as far as may be, by the consent of all, or at least by the consent of as many as may be gotten. And therefore it draweth much the obedience of the subjects of this realm, that the statutes, whereby the realm is governed, pass by the consent of the most part of it, whilst they be made by them whom the rest put in trust, and choose for that purpose, being as it were all their acts.[101]

---

100. Pearson, p. 45 quoting the *Works of John Whitgift*, volume 1, 372.
101. Pearson, p. 44, quoting the *Works of John Whifgift*, volume 1, 370.

Clearly, the consent of the governed, both in ecclesiastical and political spheres, was a hallmark of Cartwright's theory of legal and political sovereignty.[102] Jeremiah Burroughes, an influential commentator on the Book of Ezekiel, supported Cartwright's viewpoint when he wrote that no Christian was bound to obey a government "that he no way ... hath ... yielded consent unto."[103]

CONCLUSION

Modern adherents of Calvinistic theology may mourn the passing of the Puritan era. But, as Harold J. Berman of Harvard remarks, a future focus is in order:

> Merely to mourn the passing of an era would, of course, be foolish. Since there is no going back, the important question is, "How shall we go forward?" By retracing the experience through which we arrived at our present predicament, can we find some guidelines, and some resources, that may help us to overcome the obstacles that block our way to the future?[104]

---

102. There were clear limitations to the application of this principle. Cromwell, for instance, demonstrated no concern regarding the consent of Catholic Ireland when he instituted rule by the sword. The northern province, Ulster, openly embraced Puritanism while the southern provinces remained Papist. Cromwell held the Papists to be heretics and idolaters unworthy of any role in self-government. Further, Cromwell's subjugation of the Irish Papists was so severe that for decades the most fearful imprecation the Irish could hurl at each other was "the curse of Cromwell be upon you." John Stephen Flynn, *The Influence of Puritanism on the Political and Religious Thought of the English* (New York: E.P. Dutton, 1920), p. 93.

103. Jeremiah Burroughes, as quoted by Paul S. Seaver, *Journal of Church and State*, Volume 26, Number 1, Winter 1984, p. 136. Seaver quotes Donald and Keith Thomas, ed., *Puritans and Revolutionaries: Essays in Seventeenth-Century History Presented to Christopher Hill* (Oxford: Clarendon Press, Oxford University Press, 1982).

104. Berman, p. 42.

A FOCUS ON PROCEDURAL LAW IN THE CALVINISTIC REFORMATION IN NEW ENGLAND

The Role of Judge Samuel Sewall in the Salem Witch Trials

Samuel Sewall was perhaps the most famous judge of the American Puritan era. His views were recorded in voluminous courts records, including the infamous Salem witch trials, his diaries, and his numerous tracts.[1] Born in 1674, he was commissioned as judge in May 4, 1691, with these words, "let us serve our generation according to the Will of God, and afterwards fall asleep."[2] After he "fell asleep," however, history awoke to render a verdict on his role in the Salem witch trials.

---

1. See, for example, Suffolk County Probate Court, Province of the Massachusetts-Bay in New England: *Samuel Sewall Esq.; Judge for the Probate of Wills, and Granting Letters of Administration, with the County of Suffolk; Purposes, God Willing, to Wait upon that Business, at his Dwelling House in Boston, Every Second Day of the Week* (Boston: Bartholomew Green, 1715).

2. Ola Elizabeth Winslow, *Samuel Sewall of Boston* (New York: The Macmillan Company, 1964), Prologue.

INTRODUCTION: THE MANNER AND CONTENT OF SEWALL'S PUBLIC CONFESSION IN THE WITCH TRIALS

THE "HOW" OF THE CONFESSION
—The Manner of Sewall's Recanting

Into the ivy-covered cedar meeting house of South Church of Boston Judge Samuel Sewall entered to experience a defining moment in his career in jurisprudence. Sewall passed his written confession to one of the Puritan ministers, then proceeded to take his seat in the pew as he was accustomed. As the minister began to read the confession, Sewall stood up in the presence of the congregation. The confession, read aloud by the minister, implored forgiveness from his on-looking peers. Sewall's role in the condemnation of twenty souls in Salem's witch trials enslaved him in wrenching guilt.[3] His chosen means of catharsis was public recantation. What motivated the recantation? Was the recantation merely a religious phenomenon or a catharsis reasonably explained by the science of psychology? Or, does an analysis of Sewall's act require an intersection of the disciplines? Although historians chronicle Sewall's recanting, historians appear reticent to analyze the mindset from which the recantation derives.

THE "WHAT" OF THE CONFESSION
—The Written Recantation

At the crucial turning point in his social existence, Sewall, at age eighteen, perhaps redeemed himself from the harshest verdict of history when he stood before Boston's South Church while his words were read aloud to his peers:

> Samuel Sewall, sensible of the reiterated strokes of God upon himself and family; and being sensible, that as to the guilt contracted upon the opening of the late

---

3. Mary Caroline Crawford, *The Romance of Old New England Churches* (Boston: L.C. Page & Company, 1904), p. 101.

A FOCUS ON PROCEDURAL LAW IN THE CALVINISTIC REFORMATION

commission of Oyer and Terminer at Salem (to which the order for this day relates) he is, upon many accounts, more concerned than any that he knows of, desires to take the blame and shame of it, asking pardon of men, and especially desiring prayers that God, who has an unlimited authority, would pardon that sin and all other his sins, personal and relative; and according to his infinite benignity, and sovereignty, not visit the sin of him, or of any other, upon himself or any of his, nor upon the land. But that He would powerfully defend him against all temptations to sin, for the future and vouchsafe him the efficacious, saving conduct of his word and spirit.

Sewall was alone among the judges in this confession. Later the same year, Salem jurors asked public forgiveness along with several ministers.[4] Under no ecclesiastical stricture, canon law, or coercion Sewall voluntarily humbled himself before peers over whom he was promoted as judge. His lonely abasement self-inflicted, he bowed into the posture of a confessor.

ANALYSIS: THE "WHY" OF THE CONFESSION — SEWALL'S MOTIVATION

Unfortunately, no extant work adequately delves into the motivating forces which culminated in Judge Samuel Sewall's break from his fellow jurists to admit he committed irreversible error in Salem—he could not bring back the innocent he condemned. Neither religious dogma, theological formulae, nor modern psychoanalytic matrices can fully label every rubric in the human psyche. The separate disciplines of religion, ethics, and psychology each fall short of a full purview of Sewall's motivation to lay himself bare before his peers. The answer is not "either, or" but "both, and"—the disciplines of psychology, ethics, and religion intersect to disclose Sewall's motivation as an outworking of his whole person. His act of public confession on January 14, 1696, in Boston's

---

4. Theodore Benson Strandness, Samuel Sewall: a Puritan Portrait (East Lansig: Michigan State University Press, 1967) p. 76.

South Church was an outcropping of religious, moral, and psychological seeds. Sewall's confession derived from the intersection of the religious, moral, and psychological dimensions of his psyche.

THE "WHO" OF THE CONFESSION
—Sewall's Psychological, Moral, and Religious Underpinnings

His Critics and His Character

Sewall had critics—they accused him being "commonplace," "mercenary," "selfish," "sordid," especially in marriage matches. Chamberlain, who wrote the lengthiest biography of Sewall, defends Sewall on every charge. Sewall's uncommon character, the character to swallow his pride by voluntarily admitting wrongdoing before his peers, was self-evident. Although Sewall was rich by the standards of his day, he loved money no more than "most people around him." Further, he demonstrated the same frugality of his New England associates. Moreover, the concern for the violation of the rights of the falsely accused is anything but selfish. Chamberlain applies a maxim of La Rochefoucauld to Sewall—"seeking one's own, careful of the rights of others, is never selfishness." Regarding Sewall's marriage, he married rich, being rich. This was, Chamberlain defends, the custom of the times.[5] The Puritan vernacular of his age codifies the spirit of Sewall's diaries—"he was a man in whom grace and nature had long striven together for mastery, and that each had several falls."[6] Sewall was far from perfect, but no record implies that he was socially dysfunctional. Accordingly, social dysfunction was not the motivation of his public confession.

---

5. N. H. Chamberlain, *Samuel Sewall and the World He Lived In* (Boston: De Wolfe, Fiske & Company, 1898), p. 307.

6. *Ibid.*, p. 304.

A FOCUS ON PROCEDURAL LAW IN THE CALVINISTIC REFORMATION

His Temperament

Sewall was an exact Puritan in deportment. In exterior, perhaps no one was more Puritan. In his college life, in council, in the meetinghouse, and in social life, he maintained a "grave, granite temper."[7] Sewall's rigidity is evidenced by his stern discipline of his children. Wendell, in his seminal work on Cotton Mather, a friend and contemporary of Sewall, cites an excerpt from Sewall's diary:

> 1692, Joseph [Sewall's eldest child] threw a knob of brass at his sister Betty on the forehead so as to make it bleed and swell; upon which, and for his playing at Prayer time, and eating when returning thanks, I whipped him pretty smartly. When I first went in he sought not to show and hide himself from me behind the head of the cradle.[8]

Despite an apparent rigid exterior, a deeper look into Sewall's psyche reveals he was far from melancholy in his temperament. Rather, Chamberlain argues "by nature Sewall was not a Puritan." Chamberlain calls Sewall a "robust Englishman; led of his blood towards good dinners, merry wassail out of deep, silver-rimmed horns, as Saxons had done long before Harold had at Hastings; fond of merrymakings; a snatched kiss under the holly; a lover of little children gleesome in the Twelfth Night dances . . ."[9] The apparent discrepancy between Sewall's exterior and interior life may reveal a studied balance—an adaptable versatile personality which suits particular social surroundings. Or, the discrepancy may reveal a personality oversensitive to surroundings, that "caves in" to various social pressures. Winslow, however, another biographer of Sewall, sees no discrepancy between his outward demeanor and apparent emotional surges. Rather, Winslow describes Sewall with a consistent, pervading optimism:

---

7. *Ibid.*, p. 306.

8. Barrett Wendell, *Cotton Mather—the Puritan Priest* (New York: Dod, Mead, and Company, 1891), pp. 30, 31.

9. N.H. Chamberlain, p. 306.

Samuel Sewall indulged in no Jeremiads.[10] He was by nature not inclined to look on the world around him with a disapproving eye. New England had been kind to him, and in his comfortable prosperity he lived on an even keel.[11]

Although Winslow's work is thorough, Winslow does not appear to penetrate the depth of Sewall's psyche as incisively as Chamberlain's. From the evidence of the criticism of Sewall's detractors, Chamberlain's record, Winslow's record, and Sewall's diaries, Sewall appears to have experienced emotional surges more extreme than average. These apparent surges, however, fall short of what the modern field of psychology would call "manic depressive." Accordingly, emotional instability was not the overriding motivation for Sewall's recantation.

His View of the Value of Human Life

Sewall's hierarchy of values prioritized life and liberty, in that order, above all others. Sewall's sense of priority of values protrudes in his diatribe against slavery, "The Selling of Joseph—A Memorial." Sewall viewed life and liberty as singular gifts of God; therefore, both life and liberty should be cherished. Liberty, "in real value next unto life" according to Sewall, should not be surrendered. Further, liberty should not be deprived from others, including slaves.[12] Sewall did, however, couch his counsel that liberty should not be voluntarily surrendered or involuntarily taken from others with the proviso "but upon the most mature considerations."[13] Mature considerations included the practice of indentured

---

10. A "Jeremiad," in Puritan parlance, was a particular variety of homily that derived from the prophet Jeremiah. As Jeremiah preached to an apostatizing Israel, Puritan ministers resorted to this variety of address to call an "apostatizing" colony to spiritual resurgence.

11. Winslow, p. 81.

12. Samuel Sewall, *The Selling of Joseph—A Memorial* (Northampton: The University of Massachusetts Press, 1969), pp. 16–17.

13. *Ibid.*

servitude and the taking of prisoners, but only in a "just" war. The legal institution of indentured servanthood allowed a party to surrender liberty for a maximum of six years in exchange for room, board, right of passage, if necessary, to the Bay Colony, and some severance compensation. Sewall's view of the taking of prisoners in a just war derived from Deuteronomic texts[14] and the Augustinian doctrine of just war.[15] Sewall's view of slave traders imaged Moses' view articulated in Exodus 21:16, "he that stealeth a man and selleth him, or if he be found in his hand, he shall surely be put to death." Sewall, like Moses, viewed slave trading as "stealing" human beings. Moses placed such high value upon human life that he prescribed the death penalty for kidnappers.[16]

Further, Sewall substantiated his opposition to slavery on theological grounds. Because Sewall presupposed that humankind stemmed from common ancestral progenitors, the biblical Adam and Eve, Sewall concluded that humankind consisted of "siblings." Siblings, sharing a universal parenthood, should respect the life and liberty of each other. "All," according to Sewall, "are cousins, and have equal right unto liberty, and all other outward comforts of life."[17] The environment, with all its bounty, "God hath given ... with all its commodities unto the sons of Adam."[18] Sewall, however, did not hold that the universal fatherhood of Adam secured, as German theologian Harnack argues, universal redemption; rather, Sewall saw biological offspring of Adam as equal before law.[19]

---

14. Deuteronomy 20:10–18.

15. For Augustine's doctrine of "just" war, see Augustine, *De Doctrina Christiana* (Turnhout: Brepols, 1982); the Puritan branch of the Protestant Reformation imported the Augustinian view of a just war.

16. For an excellent treatment of the lexicography, grammatical structure, and syntax of the Hebrew text of Exodus 21:16, see U. Cassuto, *A Commentary on the Book of Exodus* (Jerusalem: The Magnes Press, 1987).

17. Sewall, pp. 16ff.

18. *Ibid.*

19. Radical abolition, however, has not been the Reformed consensus. Slaves converted to Christ were to remain slaves, obedient to their masters (*cf.* 1 Peter 2:18).

CALVIN THE MAGISTRATE

To Sewall, every moral and legal issue was either white or black, right or wrong. Sewall approached his religious book, the Bible, with far more reverence than a corporate attorney approaches statutes on corporate law. A corporate attorney approaches statutes to interpret them in the light most favorable to his or her client; Sewall approached his religious statute book with one hermeneutic objective—to find the one "correct" interpretation. In this spirit, Sewall lays down the law from Acts 17:26–29:

> And hath made of one blood, all nations of men, for to dwell in all the face of the earth, and hath determined the time before appointed, and the bounds of their habitation: that they should seek the Lord.

Sewall compares the care that the colonists would exercise in buying and selling a horse with the care that some colonists bought slaves:

> Tis pity there should be more caution used in buying a horse than there is in purchasing men and women, whereas they are the offspring of God and their liberty is from God."[20]

Sewall forcefully warns the colonists that his religious book of legal statutes is of everlasting equity. Accordingly, Sewall sardonically warns the colonists, "caveat emptor."[21] Capital punishment underscores the atrocity of kidnapping and slavery.

> These Ethiopians, as black as they are, seeing they are the sons and daughters of the first Adam, the brethren and sisters of the last of Adam, and the offspring of God, they ought to be treated with a respect agreeable.[22]

· Such advocacy significantly repelled the tide in Massachusetts away from the institutionalization of slavery.

---

20. *Ibid.*

21. *Ibid.*

22. Samuel Sewall, *The Selling of Joseph—A Memorial* (Northampton: The University of Massachusetts Press, 1969), pp. 16–17.

A FOCUS ON PROCEDURAL LAW IN THE CALVINISTIC REFORMATION

Further, commensurate with Sewall's high view of the value of human life, at least one recorded episode implies personal compassion. Sewall displayed great compassion for John Hull, who, when King Philip's War broke out, on his own credit financed soldiers' wages and supplies. Hull died terribly in debt, his estate amounting to less than a third of the claims of his creditors.[23] Sewall apparaently helped Hull through his troubled times.

Sewall's view of the high value of human life informed his motivation to recant of his role in the Salem witch trials. Because of his high regard for human life, his tendency to dehumanize was minimal. Further, modern forces that tend to depersonalize—technology, TV, violence, and gratuitous sex—were absent from Sewall's stark culture. One of Sewall's motives to confess was his valuation of precious human life—this valuation proceeds from religious, moral, and psychological criteria.

His Epitaph

Sewall approached ethical questions from an "all or nothing" modality—moral issues were either black or white. Sewall implies his moral inflexibility:

> And therefore I am against entering into a way never yet gone it, not beaten, and therefore not likely to be the King's Highway. Innovations are to be suspected, and avoided.[24]

Although this rigidity may appear Procrustean to the modern ethicist, George Edward Ellis is correct in his praise for the stern integrity of Sewall. Sewall's tombstone inscription is fitting: "he fell asleep in full hope of a glorious resurrection through faith in Jesus Christ. Living in an age of extraordinary events and revolutions, he learnt this truth, that all is vanity which is not honest

---

23. Samuel Eliot Morison, *Builders of the Bay Colony* (Boston: Riverside Press for the Houghton Mifflin Company, 1930), p. 181.

24. *The Letter Book of Samuel Sewall*, September 5, 1724, (Boston: Massachusetts Historical Society Collection, 1886), II, 173.

CALVIN THE MAGISTRATE

..."[25] Honesty is more valuable than prestige. Sewall, by confessing publicly, evidenced he had balanced position, prestige, and power on the one hand and integrity on the other. Conclusively, he weighed a clear conscience of greater value than the security of the status quo. Sewall confessed to clear his conscience; his conscience had religious, moral, and psychological dimensions.

THE "WHY" OF THE CONFESSION
—The Function of Sewall's Perception of Religious Law

Puritanism was both personal and formal in dimension[26]—formal Puritanism is that movement in its "creeds, politics, manners,

25. George Edward Ellis, *An Address on the Life and Character of Chief-Justice Samuel Sewall: Delivered in the Old South Church, Boston, Sunday, October 26, 1884. On occasion of the erection of tablets in the Church, commemorative of its line of ministers, and of Samuel Sewall and Samuel Adams* (Boston: Press of David Clapp & Son, 1885); N.H. Chamberlain, *Samuel Sewall and the World He Lived In* (Boston: De Wolfe, Fiske & Company, 1898), p. 308. Compare Cotton Mather's eulogy for Mrs. Samuel Sewall in his sermon, *The Valley of Baca: The Divine Sovereignty, Displayed and Adored; more Particularly, in Bereaving Dispensations of the Death of Mrs. Samuel Sewall Esq.; which Befell Us, on the 19th Day, Seventh Month, 1717.*

26. What was Puritanism? Puritanism was an interdenominational movement to continue the Calvinistic Reformation of Christianity in the United Kingdom and later the British Crown colonies. Calvinistic reformers as early as John Jewell and Thomas Cartwright in the late sixteenth century were English Puritan luminaries. Key seventeenth-century luminaries included Stephen Charnock, Thomas Goodwin, John Owen, and Thomas Boston. Puritans sought an intellectual, moral, and spiritual cleanup of institutionalized Christianity. Their standard of purity was the Bible, solely the Old and New Testaments without the Apocrypha of Catholicism. Their comprehensive but concise articulation of ideology was the Westminster Confession of Faith, written by a symposium of 120 Puritan scholars from 1643 to 1648. Although this Confession formulated a Presbyterian church government, Separatist Puritans, Congregationalist Puritans, and Anglican Puritans embraced the basic theology of this Confession. The end of Cromwell's Lord's Protectorate in 1660 marked the end of Puritan hegemony over British political, social, and ecclesiastical institutions. Although Jonathan Edwards, whose revivalist influence began in earnest in 1739, has been designated the last American Puritan, Puritan hegemony over Massachusetts reached a nadir in the 1690s, when some Puritan ideologues migrated from Massachusetts to Connecticut

and its other visible on-goings."²⁷ Personal Puritanism comprises the same formal elements found in the individual, "as elements of character are colored by the party's personality."²⁸ A key component of the Puritan political agenda was religious substantive law. Religious substantive law played a significant role in informing Sewall's conscience of the evil of his contribution to the Salem witch trials.

Substantive Puritan Law

The Massachusetts Bay Colony's legal development was unfettered by the hostilities of the Puritan revolution in England. Unhampered by the factionalism, the colony became an apotheosis of a society structured by religious law. More than anywhere else, the Puritan concept of the reformation of the world led directly to a theory and practice of law as a means of religious transformation of society. In England in the 1640s and 1650s, for instance, over ten thousand pamphlets were published arguing for legal reforms.²⁹ New England Puritans carried the torch of legal reform further than their counterparts across the Atlantic.

As a source of law, the New England Puritans viewed to their sacred writings:

> Whatsoever ordinance of the Old Testament is not repealed in the New Testament, as peculiar to the Jewish Paedagogie, but was of moral and perpetual equity, the same binds us in these days, and is to be accounted the revealed will of God in all ages, though it be not particularly and expressly mentioned in the writings of the New

---

to found Yale.

27. N. H. Chamberlain, *Samuel Sewall and the World He Lived In* (Boston: De Wolfe, Fiske & Company, 1898), p. 305.

28. *Ibid.*

29. Sermon to the House of Commons, 1641, quoted in Rosenstock-Huessy, *Out of the Revolution: The Autobiography of Western Man* 291 (1938), as quoted by Harold J. Berman, "Religious Foundations of Law in the West: An Historical Perspective," *Journal of Law and Religion*, Volume 1, Number 1, Summer 1983, p. 30. Berman, p. 30.

Testament . . . the Scriptures of the New Testament do speak little in these cases; only the Scripture of the Old Testament do give direction and light about them.[30]

When Sewall stood on January 14, 1696, while his confession was read, he stood not only a religious figure but also a legal one. The religious law that had shaped his professional training at Harvard College and his jurisprudential stance had moral "teeth" to chew on his entire psyche. Religious law played a part in Sewall's motivation to stand and retract his illegitimate juridical opinions. Sewall's response to the morality of religious law propelled him to leave the "slavery" of unlawfulness into the "liberty of lawfulness."

The Cohesive New England Social Order

When the Puritans erected their "city upon a hill" in the 1620s, they established a colony distinct in political texture from than the other colonies. Conflicting interest groups in New York and Pennsylvania vied for their interests in the political and economic arena.[31] The southern royal colonies endured class violence and a subsistence crisis. Further, fear of the growing black population in the south solidified the white aristocracy.[32] Social unrest, however, was rare in the Bay Colony; rather, Massachusetts was remarkably cohesive socially. Differences revolved around religious issues, such as the Half-Way Covenant, and policy concerns, such as the regulation of navigation to appease the British Crown.[33] Biblical law provided a social emulsifier for the colony. Additionally, the comprehensiveness and severity of biblical law raised the moral concerns of the colonists.

---

30. *An Apology of the Churches in New England for Church-Covenant* (London, 1643), p. 8, as quoted by John F. Wilson, *Pulpit in Parliament* (Princeton: University Press, 1969), p. 143.

31. William Pencak, *War, Politics, and Revolution in Provincial Massachusetts* (Boston: Northeastern University Press, 1981), p. 2.

32. *Ibid.*

33. William Pencak, *War, Politics, and Revolution in Provincial Massachusetts* (Boston: Northeastern University Press, 1981), pp. 2-6.

A FOCUS ON PROCEDURAL LAW IN THE CALVINISTIC REFORMATION

As an emulsifier, biblical law pervaded the school system in Massachusetts. Since the ideological indoctrination began at an early age for all children, the society developed an ideological commonality that bound the colony together. Unlike Pennsylvania, where the Dutch Reformed taught their children in Dutch, Quakers taught their children according to their creed, and the Swedish Covenant churches taught their children according to their creed and in their language, only a small minority of the Massachusetts colonists differed from the Puritan creed and all spoke English. Commonality in creed and language was unique to Massachusetts.[34]

January 14, 1696, was day of contrition for the whole colony—a day of "solemn fasting and prayer" for what might have been done amiss "in the late tragedy, raised among us by Satan and his instruments, through the awful judgment of God."[35] The colonist Sewall was not only a religious being but a social being. Being emulsified with the homogeneous Puritan society, he became estranged from his own people by what he done to them in the Salem witch trials. Separated from his society, he sought to tear down the barrier between himself and his society by means of public confession. Fundamental to every human being is the need to belong—essential to Sewall's sense of belonging was his public confession. Public confession was a purgation of the horror of being alone—a way to blast away the lonely past of sitting in judgment on one's people and betraying them by putting their innocent to death.

---

34. Thomas Jefferson Wertenbaker, *The Puritan Oligarchy—The Founding of American Civilization* (New York: Charles Scriber's Sons, 1947).

35. Theodore Benson Strandness, *Samuel Sewall: A Puritan Portrait* (East Lansig: Michigan State University Press, 1967) p. 76.

THE "IN RE" OF THE CONFESSION
—The Tragic Superstitions

Shakespeare's depiction of the three witches in *MacBeth* may appear entertaining to the modern reader, but to the colonists of Massachusetts Bay, the depiction was not far from reality:

> First Witch:
> >Round about the cauldron go;
> >In the poisn'd entrails throw.—
> >Toad, that under the cold stone
> >Days and nights hast thirty-one
> >Sweltered venom sleeping got
> >Boil thou first i' the charmed pot.
>
> All:
> >Double, double, toil and trouble;
> >Fire, burn; and, cauldron, bubble.
>
> MacBeth:
> >Infected be the air whereon they ride,
> >And damned all those that trust them.

N.H. Chamberlain, using the caldron and condiments as a conceit, relates that:

> . . . into that Salem caldron, out of the hands of that Puritan age and people, were poured some of the most mixed, unreachable, and poisonous motives of which probably the human mind, in its most occult relationship to the human body, has as yet shown itself capable of emitting.[36]

Tragically, the bubbles in Shakespeare's portrayal turned to blood, and the "smoke of this witches' incense" casts a dark cloud over New England's history.[37] According to this lore, women had "teats" on their bodies which imps or animal "familiars" came to suck at night. These "familiars" came in the form of cats, birds,

---

36. N. H. Chamberlain, *Samuel Sewall and the World He Lived in* (Boston: De Wolfe, Fiske & Company, 1898), p. 158.

37. *Ibid.*

dogs, and snakes.[38] In the same vein, Ewen introduces his excellent work on *Witchcraft and Demonianism* as follows:

> Of wrathful witches this same pamphlet tels,
> How most of all on simple folke they worke.
> What wonders to, they may atchiue by spels,
> God weede them out in euery cell they lurke,
> God weeds them out, but Satan stil doth hatch
> fresh Imps, whereby of al sorts he may catch.[39]

The belief in the existence of witchcraft, and accusations commensurate with this belief, derived from several sources. First, they derived from direct biblical teaching. John Wesley would later say in 1768 that "giving up of witchcraft is in effect giving up the Bible."[40] Sir William Blackstone, chronicler of the common law, wrote in 1765 that "in general there has been such a thing as witchcraft, though one cannot give credit to any particular modern instance of it." Second, false accusations of corrupt ministers perpetuated the belief in witchcraft. Third, medical doctors ascribed some diseases to supernatural origin, which gave rise to accusations of witchcraft. Fourth, the statutory law that forbade witchcraft obviously presupposed its existence. Fifth, misunderstanding in cause of great mortality of children and livestock; often, such losses were ascribed to witchcraft. Sixth, demented individuals would sometimes "confess" to being witches. Seventh, the populace would hold mental degenerates as credible sources.[41]

Although ideologically Sewall believed in witches, much of the lore of the day went far beyond the sacred writings he held dear. Sewall, in recanting, returned from a line he had crossed from his religion into superstition. His refusal to hear "spectral" evidence—that is, testimony of sighted phantasms, visages, and

---

38. David D. Hall, *Witchhunting in Seventeenth Century New England* (Boston: Northeastern University Press, 1991), p. 6.

39. C. L'Estrange Ewen, *Witchcraft and Demonianism* (London: Heath Cranton, Ltd., 1933), preface.

40. John Wesley, *The Works of John Wesley*, vol. 4, p. 60.

41. C. L'Estrange Ewen, *Witchcraft and Demonianism* (London: Heath Cranton, Ltd., 1933), p. 138.

specters—demonstrates his departure from superstitious lore. Sewall's confession marked a raising of evidentiary standards above the fantastic and ridiculous.

THE "IN RE" OF THE CONFESSION
—Group Hysteria

The sociopolitical community was ripe for some outlet for pent-up group anxiety. With the loss of the colony's charter, a communal apprehension descended upon the colony's group consciousness. The "sore" and "apprehensive" community was ripe for an "acting out." The psychology of the community fixated upon a simplistic "solution" to the anxiety. Eradicate the evil in the colony; surgically remove the tumor from the sick social organism! If the cause of God's "curse" was found and removed, the community would "feel better." The community was feeling "out of joint" because their political future hung in the balance, the community sought a simplistic "out"—"Burn the witches!" Out of a slough of an unknown transition, a "good" mob materialized to blame the "evil" Satan worshipers.[42] The Salem witch burning was a fixation hysteria *en masse*.

Further, sociopolitical community had evolved. A new generation of Puritans had been hardened by King Philip's War. The maneuvers of that war brought many of the new generation in touch with the uncivil cruelties of the wilderness. Backsliding into a mild barbarism forged by war and wilderness, the new generation was far more prone to violence than the earlier. Additionally, the new generation suffered from less education than their forebears.[43]

The sociopolitical community was spiritually high strung. Puritanism, with its incessant introspection, produced a mind taut with spiritual tension. The vibrations of the spiritually taut psyche of the community were unnaturally acute.[44] High-strung tem-

---

42. *Cf.* Chamberlain, p. 161.
43. *Ibid.*
44. *Ibid.*

peraments are given to behavioral extremes and perceptual biases. Spiritually, the witch trials were an "honest but fierce outburst of fanaticism."[45] Religious "mobocracy" is a poor substitute for good government.

The sociopolitical community was corporately paranoid. At Gloucester, for instance, the citizens actually shut themselves up in their fortress to prepare for an imminent attack by demons in force. Any accusation was equivalent to an indictment. Accused parties were guilty until proven guilty. Indictments were equivalent to sentences. Those awaiting trial were denied bail.[46]

Mob mania is a frightening phenomenon. Consider Hitler and the Jews. The demonized and consequently persecuted minority becomes an opposite "pole" for the tyrannical majority. Through manipulation by group defamation, Nazi society became polarized—"us" against "them." "Because 'they' are evil, 'we' must be good. Because 'they' are demonic, 'we' must be angelic." The minority's scarlet letters and albatrosses as neck ornaments make the majority feel "good." Group paranoia became the cement to glue together a homogeneous Nazi society. The threat, real or imagined, of a common enemy fosters strong alliances. Tragically, the Puritan society degenerated into mania of group paranoia. The paranoia aroused Puritan society to look for a common enemy, even if there was none—consider the barricading of the stockade at Gloucester from the advancing demons. Some societies degenerate to the left, disintegrating into anarchy. Other societies degenerate to the right, tyrannizing minorities.

What sick, warped minds like Chief Justice William Stoughton's may do! Although Sewall joined the bandwagon mania commandeered by Stoughton, at least Sewall later came to his senses. Sewall's return to sanity underscores the depth of the evil of character assassination, smear campaigns, "black-balling," false accusation, and prejudiced jurists. Ignorance, error, prejudice, and bigotry combined into a leviathan of starved terror, seeking whom it might devour.

45. *Ibid.*
46. *Ibid.*, p. 163.

CALVIN THE MAGISTRATE

The name "Reginald Denny" has become a synonym for "mob hysteria" of late, but history is replete with group hysteria phenomena.[47] Sewall, caught up in the whirlwind of the Salem phenomenon, returned to his senses. A return to sanity motivated his public confession.

THE "IN RE" OF THE CONFESSION
—Mock Examination of Witnesses

The following is an example of interrogation by Simon Willard of an alleged "witch" common to the "trials." In the following "fact-finding proceeding," a child of eight years of age is questioned:

> Question: how long have you been a witch? Ever since I was six years old. how old are you now? Near eight years old; brother Richard says I shall be eight years old in November next. Who made you a witch? My mother. She made me set my hand to a book. How did you set your hand to it? I touched it with my fingers and the book was red; the paper of it was white. She said she had never seen "the Black Man, "—i. e., the Devil,—but she had touched the book, and so Become the Devil's own in Andres Foster's pasture, and that her mother, cousin, and aunt among others were there.
>
> Question: What did they promise to give you?
>
> Answer: A black dog. Did the dog ever come to you? No. But you said you saw a cat once—what did that say

---

47. An illuminating study of hypochondriacal delusions is E. Steinebrunner, Archiv-fur-Psychiatrie-und Nervenkrankeheiten, 1976 Vol. 222(1) 47–60.

Conducting a meta-analysis of 101 cases dating from 1973 and 100 cases dating from 1912, Steinebrunner concluded: first, delusions as to reference, religion, and persecution were stable. Second, over time, hypochondriacal delusions significantly increase while megalomania and erotomania decrease. Third, with increasing age, delusions of special descent, paranoid identity change, and erotamania decrease. Further, after age thirty, delusions of special descent, paranoid identity change, querulant paranoia, and erotamania did not occur. *Ibid.* Individual hypochondriacal delusions combined with group hysteria could produce unique phenomenon. Group or social hypochondria may apply to the psychology of the Bay Colony in 1692.

A FOCUS ON PROCEDURAL LAW IN THE CALVINISTIC REFORMATION

> to you? It said it would tear me in pieces if I would not set my hand to the book. She said further, her mother baptized her, and the Devil or "black man" was not there as she saw, and her mother said when she baptized her, "thou art mine forever and ever, Amen."

But Martha Currier defended herself with an honest woman's anger. She denied everything in every particular; that she had ever seen or dealt with the Devil, or hurt any one. She said to the magistrates, "It is a shameful thing that you should mind these folks who are out of their wits;" and turning to her accusers, now resting from their fits a little, cried, "You lie! I am wronged." Her courage threw the great crowd into an uproar; and the record closes in these words: "The tortures of the afflicted were so great that there was no enduring of it, so that she was ordered away, to be bound hand and foot with all expedition; the afflicted in the meanwhile, almost killed, to the great trouble of all spectators, magistrates, and others."[48]

Moreover, the magistrates were told by one of the witnesses, out of court, the accused confessed to her that "she had been a witch 40 years."[49] She also deposed that she afflicted persons by pinching them, that she went to them not in her body but in her spirit, and that her mother carried her to the place of mischief. Being further asked, "How did your mother carry you when she was in prison?" she replied, "She came like a black cat." How did you know it was your mother? The cat told me so; that she was my mother.[50] The "confession" of another infant of the same mother runs thus: "Have you been in the Devil's snare? Yes. How long has your brother been a witch? Near a month. How long have you been a witch? Not long. She afterwards added to her last answer, 'about five weeks.' "[51] This kind of travesty literally led innocent souls to their deaths.

---

48. Chamberlain, p. 164.
49. *Ibid.*, p. 164.
50. *Ibid.*, p. 164.
51. *Ibid.*

CALVIN THE MAGISTRATE

The legitimacy that fueled the orgy of hangings dissipated with time. "Spectral" evidence is testimony pertaining to specters. Specters are visible incorporeal spirits, especially ones of a terrifying nature.[52] Spectrology, "the study of ghosts, phantoms, and apparitions," was more the source of the legitimacy than the Congregationalists' theology.[53]

Thomas Brattle, for instance, was not in minority in 1693. In his famous letter dated October 8, he wrote:

> Those Wenches being present, who plaid their juggling tricks, falling down, crying out, and staring in Peoples Faces; the Magistrates demanded of them several times, who it was of all the People in the Room that hurt them? One of these Accusers pointed several times at one Captain Hill, there present, but spake nothing; the same Accuser had a Man standing at her back to hold her up; he stooped down to her Ear, then she cried out, Aldin, Aldin afflicted her; one of the Magistrates asked her if she had ever seen Aldin, she answered no, he asked her how she knew it was Aldin? She said, the Man told her so.[54]

---

52. *The Random House Dictionary of the English Language*, Second Edition, (New York: Random House, 1987.), p. 1832.

53. *Ibid.*, p. 1833; at the execution of George Burrough, John Willard, John Proctor, Martha Carrier and George Jacobs, several ministers were present with Sewall—Cotton Mather, Simms, Hale, Noyes, and Chiever. When the number of accusations grew to include more and more persons of good reputation and upright life, even the wife of the Governor, Mather concluded that "many unsearchable cheats were interwoven into the doleful business." Mather lamented that "a good name, obtained by a good life, should not be lost by mere spectral accusations." The notorious Special Court of Oyer and Terminer was disbanded in October of 1696; the Superior Court replacing it on January 3, 1697, formally adopted a more sane evidentiary standard. When the Superior Court was asked by the jury what weight should spectral evidence carry, the Superior Court responded "as much as Chips in Wort"—less than worthlessness. Theodore Benson Strandness, *Samuel Sewall: A Puritan Portrait* (East Lansig: Michigan State University Press, 1967), p. 74; Cotton Mather, *Magnalia Christi Americana* (Carlisle, PA.: Banner of Truth Trust, reprint edition), I, 212.

54. Bernard Rosenthal, *Salem Story—Reading the Witch Trials of 1692* (Boston: Cambridge University Press, 1993), pp. 186-87.

A FOCUS ON PROCEDURAL LAW IN THE CALVINISTIC REFORMATION

Brattle ridicules the whole episode and remarks "that the reasonable part of the world, when acquainted herewith, will laugh at the demonstration, and conclude that the said S.G. are actually possessed, at least, with ignorance and folly." Further, Brattle singles out the Reverend Nicholas Noyes for being so gullible.[55]

Clearly, Sewall had much to burden his conscience—hearsay, reported phantasms, imaginations, and outright lies. The discovery phase of these investigations turned fact-finding into a nauseating farce. Sewall sought to purge his conscience of a travesty of evidentiary analysis.

THE "IN RE" OF THE CONFESSION
—The Barbaric Torture

The history of the means to extract confessions is sordid. Although the Anglo-American evolution is less shocking than the Continental, violent practices to induce confession on both sides of the Channel would make even the most extreme Christian sect shudder. The means regularly sanctioned to acquire confessions borders on the barbaric.[56] The suggested figure of 300,000 executions throughout Europe and the British Isles during the seventeenth century is perhaps conservative. But the horror of nineteen

---

55. *Ibid.*, p. 188.

56. H. Richard Uviller, Evidence from the Mind of the Criminal Suspect: A Reconsideration of the Current Rules of Access and Restraint, 87 Colum. L. Rev. 1137, 1140, October 1987. The goals of limitation of coercion, physical or otherwise, is to ensure that confessions are reliable expressions of the truth. The privilege against self-incrimination "tap the roots of the basic stream of religious and political principle." This privilege sets limits to the individual's attornment to the sate. And further, it philosophically upholds the principle of individual autonomy by "equalizing" the individual and the state. Barry C. Feld, Criminalizing Juvenile Justice: Rules of Procedure for the Juvenile Court, 69 Minn. L. Rev. 141, 157 (1984). Feld continues his discussion of the impropriety of requiring an accused party to testify against themselves: "one of its purposes is to prevent the state, whether by force or by psychological domination, from overcoming the mind and will of the person under investigation and depriving him of the freedom to decide whether to assist the state in securing his conviction." *Id.* at 157.

CALVIN THE MAGISTRATE

deaths on the gallows and one under heavy stones in New England is small in proportion.[57]

By English law, an adult male might be "pressed" to the point of death. The unfortunate male who refused to respond to an arraignment with the plea of "yea" or "nay" would be brought three times before the sentencing court and told the penalty. If he remained recalcitrant, the prisoner would be bound hand and foot on the floor of his cell. Heavy iron weights were put on his body. The first day he was to receive three morsels of the worst moldy bread. The second day he was to receive three cups of stagnant water found nearest the prison walls. But, each day weights were added to his body until he was literally crushed to death. The Puritans maintained an ironic grim thrift even in the cost of imprisonment and torture. The prisoner or the prisoner's estate was charged for the torture implements, room, board, security expenses, and court fees.[58] Unfortunately, the Puritans again forgot their Bibles—Moses prescribed no prisons, only temporary custody in six cities of refuge for those accused of murder. Any other malefactor, according to Moses, was either fined, flogged, or suffered capital punishment.

The English courts utilized torture from 1540 to 1640 at least in 81 cases.[59] The use of torture ended, however, with the advent of the Puritan revolution in 1640. But during this period, no privilege against self-incrimination was created.[60] With a rash of sexual immorality in the early 1640s, in the winter of 1641–42, Governor Bellingham sought counsel from ministers and local magistrates on use of "violence" to compel confession. Bellingham asked, "May a magistrate extract a confession of a capital crime from a suspected and an accused person?" Ralph Partrich answered in

---

57. Ola Elizabeth Winslow, *Samuel Sewall of Boston* (New York: The Macmillan Company, 1964), p. 114.

58. Chamberlain, pp. 171–72.

59. John H. Langbein, "The Historical Origins of the Privilege against Self-incrimination at Common Law," 92 Mich. L. Rev. 1047, 1085, March 1994.

60. *Id.* at 1100–1102.

A FOCUS ON PROCEDURAL LAW IN THE CALVINISTIC REFORMATION

terms consistent with common law and Congregationalist Puritan dogma:

> I conceive that a magistrate is bound, by careful examination of circumstances and within probabilities, to sift the accused; and by force of argument to draw him to an acknowledgment of the truth. But he may not extract a confession of a capital crime from a suspected person by any violent means, whether it be by an oath imposed or by any punishment inflicted or threatened to be inflicted, for so he may draw forth and acknowledgment of a crime from a fearful innocent. If guilty, he shall be compelled to be his own accuser, when no other can, which is against the rule of justice.[61]

Bradford transcribed excerpts from his response and that of Charles Chauncy into his manuscript. To Bradford and the others involved, the issue was more pressing than academic. September of 1642, Thomas Granger of Duxbury was executed on his own confession to repeated acts of bestiality.[62]

---

61. *Id.* at 1102.

62. *Id.* at 1102–3; William Bradford, *Of Plymouth Plantation, 1620–1647*, at 317–18, (Samuel E. Mirison ed., 1952); Wigmore asserted that the maxim nemo tenetur was an old and established ecclesiastical practice. John H. Wigmore, Nemo tenetur Seipsum Prodere, 5 Harv. L. Rev. 71, 83 (1891). In 1532, the Archbishop of Canterbury examined John Lambert for heresy, of which he was later convicted. Lambert argued that "no man is bound to accuse himself." In 1533, Parliament enacted a new statute on the punishment of treason, "any persons presented or indicted of any heresy, or duly accused by two lawful witnesses, may be cited, arrested, or taken by a church official who sat in ecclesiastical court, other of the King's subjects to answer in open court. In 1537 the statute was amended under Edward, providing that no person "shall be indicted, arraigned, condemned or convicted" for treason unless he be "accused by two sufficient and lawful witnesses, or shall willingly without violence confess the same." In 1584, Puritans Wiggenton and Blake refused to answer the questions of the High Commission. Wiggenton states that he had not received a copy of the charges of the names of his accusers. Blake responded with a lecture about compulsory self-incrimination. *Id.* at 119.

In 1587, Henry Barrow, a separatist leader, insisted on the right to face the witnesses against him. *Id.* at 119. In 1588, hard-hitting, easy to read, pseudonymously written (the author never discovered, called himself "Martin Marprellate") tracts appeared which ridiculed prelacy. One suspected author was

When the judges of Salem led by Chief Justice Stoughton reverted to physical torture, they retrogressed legally and morally.[63] Sewall, regressing with them, realized his folly. Accordingly, Sewall's confession proceeded from colossal dimensions of moral and legal error. A public purgation of his errors was Sewall's chosen means of retraction.

THE "IN RE" OF THE CONFESSION
—The Possible Gender Factor

The evil of witch hunting had a tragic gender dimension. Four times as many women as men were accused of witchcraft. Further, the men so accused were often sons or husbands of alleged witches. The fullest chronicle of gender-biased patterns is Carol Karlsen's *The Devil in the Shape of a Woman*. Women were particularly vulnerable because of the particular social order of the Bay Colony. Legal, political, ideological, and economic authority rested exclusively with men.[64]

A striking case of theological blame shifting was Zachary Dibble of Stamford Connecticut in 1669. Sarah Dibble accused

---

Wiggenton, who when arrested refused to answer on ground that "I account it as unnatural a thing for me to answer against myself, as to thrust a knife into my thigh. *Id.* at 120.

In 1580, another suspected author, John Udall, may have been the first person to claim a right of silence in a common law proceeding. John H. Langbein, "The Historical Origins of the Privilege against Self-incrimination at Common Law," 92 Mich. L. Rev. 1047, 1085, March 1994.

63. The Chief Justice at Salem was a strident, hardened Puritan version of, perhaps, Senator Helms. His jury instructions are particularly noteworthy: "the Devil could not appear in the form of any one who was not in league with him. If followed, therefore, as the Devil had appeared in the form of many of the accused, according to the eye-witnesses there, the defendants must be guilty." Stoughton maintained the righteousness of his cause to the end, resigning rather than compromise his personal jihad against the demonized minority. Like Lt. William Cally after My Lai, Stoughton maintained not only his innocence but his righteousness. N. H. Chamberlain, *Samuel Sewall and the World He Lived In* (Boston: De Wolfe, Fiske & Company, 1898), p. 169.

64. David D. Hall, *Witchhunting in Seventeenth Century New England* (Boston: Northeastern University Press, 1991): 6-7.

A FOCUS ON PROCEDURAL LAW IN THE CALVINISTIC REFORMATION

Zachary of physical abuse but Zachary denied, claiming that her bruises were the result of acute "witchcraft." Although the court rejected his counterclaim, Zachary's allegation implies how commonplace the witch labeling was.[65]

The gender factor raises yet another blemish on the ugly head of the witch hunts. Although Sewall, as a man of his day, may not have been cognizant of particular injustices to women, his confession belies an awareness of the injustices done to humanity as a whole. From this sordid episode, Sewall sought catharsis when he stood before South Church in Boston to recant.

CONCLUSION: THE INTERPLAY OF RELIGIOUS, MORAL, AND PSYCHOLOGICAL FACTORS

There are no entries in Sewall's journal for the months of April, May, and June 1696, when the hysteria was at its height. Sewall's entries concerning the proceedings were few and brief but revelatory. As Chamberlain observes: "He evidently was ashamed, cast down, full of sorrow, and probably afraid of personal prosecution and loss of property and of the survivors suing for damages."[66] Sewall believed the death of several of his young children was "caused" by his role in the witch condemnations.[67]

Although Sewall confessed alone, he was not the only soul agonizing over the shedding of innocent blood. Michael Wigglesworth, for instance, expressed dire concern:

> I fear (among our many other provocations) that God hath a Controversy with us about what was done in the time of the Witchcraft. I fear that innocent blood hath been shed; and that many have had their hands defiled therewith. I believe our Godly Judges did act Conscientiously, according to what they did apprehend then to

---

65. *Id.* at 7; morally, it was fitting for Zachary to suffer the penalty for being a witch himself, presupposing, of course, his accusation was false.

66. N. H. Chamberlain, *Samuel Sewall and the World He Lived In* (Boston: De Wolfe, Fiske & Company, 1898), p. 168.

67. Chamberlain, p. 173.

be sufficient Proof: But since that, have not the Devil's impostures appeared? and that most of the Complainers and Accusers were acted by him in giving their testimonies. Be it then that it . . . was done ignorantly. Paul, a Pharisee, persecuted the church of God, shed the blood of God's saints, and yet obtained mercy, because he did it in ignorance; but how doth he bewail it, and shame himself for it before God and men afterwards.[68]

Sewall, therefore, was not alone in his strident remorse.

A profitable religious parallel in an analysis of Sewall's motivation to confess publicly is the tradition of Kenyan youths of Okiek. Kratz contrasts religious confession between Western Catholic tradition and the tradition of Okiek youths in Kenya, the final ritual component prior to the ritual climax of circumcision of the males or excision of the females. Just prior to the circumcision or excision, public confession of social debts qualifies the initiate for the ritual climax. The religious functionary presiding over the event publicly questions the initiate, then announces the "social debts" to the assembly. The interrogator then creatively recasts the "sins" of the initiate into a narrative transformation. The recasting is the symbolic ritual act of absolution of past "sins." The humiliation of the initiate before the amused assembly serves as a milestone for the initiate, purging the initiate of past sins and ushering the initiate into absolution and maturity.[69]

Kratz' study opens a window, perhaps, into Sewall's psyche. His humiliation before his peers served to purge of his past and usher him into a new era of absolution and maturity. The trauma of public humiliation[70] was not only a form of self-punishment,

---

68. Michael Wigglesworth, letter to Increase Mather in 1704, *Collections of the Massachusetts Historical Society*, vol. 8, 4th ser., p. 646; Bernard Rosenthal, *Salem Story—Reading the Witch Trials of 1692* (Boston: Cambridge University Press, 1993), p. 183.

69. Corinne A. Kratz, "Amusement and Absolution: Transforming Narratives During Confession of Social Debts," *American Anthropologist* 1991 Dec. Vol. 93(4): 826–851.

70. What stark irony to compare Sewall's humility with the attitude of many federal judges. The common adage, "you are never closer to God than

but a psychological wall erected to impede his ability to turn back and look at his ghastly past. Ultimately, however, Samuel Sewall's public confession ignited through the intersection of the religious, moral, and psychological dimensions.

---

when you are in the presence of a federal court judge sitting on the bench," rings true.

CONCLUSION

The Legacy of the Legal and Political Theory of John Calvin

Calvin's Contribution Cannot Be Ignored—By Friend or Foe
In the final analysis, the testimony of friend and foe vortex into the inescapable reality that Calvin's contribution cannot be ignored. "If I had such servants my dominion would extend from sea to sea"[1] opined Pope Pius IV, whose hegemony Calvin undermined. "Calvin . . . was a master of equivocation" repined one of his critics.[2] Conversely, disciples of Calvin's contribution speak in obverse expostulation. "I have read the fathers and the school men, and Calvin too; but I find that he that has Calvin has them all"[3] exclaimed the New England Puritan John Cotton. When he was asked why he retired later than usual, Cotton quipped, "Because I love to sweeten my mouth with a piece of Calvin before I go to sleep."[4] Friend and foe speak of Calvin in superlative terms, however, positively or negatively.

---

1. Otto Scott, "The Great Christian Revolution," in *The Great Christian Revolution—The Myths of Paganism and Arminianism* (Vallecito, Calif.: Ross House Books, 1991), p. 130.

2. Michael Walzer, *The Revolution of the Saints: A Study in the Origins of Radical Politicals* (Cambridge, Mass.: Harvard University Press, 1965), p. 23.

3. Cotton Mather, *Magnalia Christi Americana* (Hartford, 1853), I, p. 274.

4. Mather, I, p. 274.

CONCLUSION

CALVIN'S EXPANSIVE AND EXTENSIVE INFLUENCE

The contribution of Calvin was impossible to ignore not only because of its content, but also the expansive means of its communication through the printing press. The printing press was the decisive weapon of the Reformation, and for the Papacy, devastating. In various regions of Europe, the power of the press whelmed, if not overwhelmed, the power of the Papacy.[5]

CALVIN WAS AN AMALGAM OF THE INFLUENCES OF HIS DAY

The salient, even strident mark that Calvin left upon his day (1509–64) derives from forces that shaped him. First of all he was a Renaissance humanist scholar. The humanist caption *ad fontes*, or "back to the original sources," became the prime directive for the young Calvin. Not only did humanist scholarship include Latin, Greek, and Hebrew original sources, but also the Church Fathers. To the core of Calvin's "credo" . . . if Augustine had not piped, Calvin would not have danced. The Lutheran battle cry and meme, "sola scriptura," fueled his epistemology. The rhetorical burden borne by Calvin, through ceaseless advocacy, to convince that Scripture only should be religious authority, found fertile soil among the religiously disillusioned masses.[6]

---

5. *Cf.* Alister E. McGrath, *A Life of John Calvin* (Oxford, 1990) and Ronald S. Wallace, *Calvin, Geneva, and the Reformation* (Edinburgh, 1989).

6. *Cf.* William G. Naphy, *Calvin and the Consolidation of the Genevan Reformation* (Manchester, New York: Manchester University Press, 1994); Daniel Buscarlet, *International Monument of Reformation: A Short Outline* (Genieve: Editions l'Eau Vive, 196–); *Monument International de la Reformation a Geneve* (Geneve, Imprimerie Atar, 1909?); Henri Naef, *Les origines dal refomea Geneve, la cit'e des 'ev'eques, l'humanimse, les signes preecurseurs; publie par la Societe d'histoire et d'archeologie de geneve, avec le concours de la Societe auxiliarie des sceince et des arts* (Paris, E. Droz, Geneva, A. Jullien, 1936); for a helpful bibliography, see Theophile Dufour, *Notice Bibliographique sur le Catechisme et la Confession de foi de Calvin (1537) et sur les autres livres imprimes a Geneve et a Neuchatel dans les priemers temps de la Reforme (1533–40)*

CALVIN THE MAGISTRATE

THE EXCURSUS ON THE SALEM WITCH TRIALS ILLUSTRATES A GAPING HOLE OF LACK OF REFORM IN THE LAW OF EVIDENCE

Gaping in Calvin's legal legacy is the lack of reform as to a reasonable law of evidence. Calvin did not proffer reform of the law of evidence significantly. "Spectral evidence" involving unconfirmed, unilateral visions, even apparitions, of demonic appearances, the norm in Europe, resulted in judicially sanctioned murder in the New England witch trials at Salem. Genevan law, under the influence Calvin's ministrations, did not evolve significantly. "Thou shalt not bear false witness against thy neighbor," the Ninth Commandment of Moses was dishonored by the erroneous rule of evidence allowing for unilateral, fantastical allegations. Under the law of Moses, two or three witnesses were required for a prosecution of murder (cf. Deut. 17:6; 19:15). The Apostle Paul expanded the parameters of evidentiary considerations in 2 Corinthians 13:1, ". . . at the mouth of two or three witnesses shall every word be established." The line drawn between the Salem trials and Genevan trials is not long—although the witch trials at Salem rose, or rather descended, to notoriety (and infamy) an attorney transferring bar membership from one city to the other would not have had to attend an extensive crash course on the law of evidence. To be sure, Calvin is not responsible for murders in Salem. However, the point to be made is that Calvin's legal legacy did not include a significant evolution of the law of evidence, as demonstrated by the almost maniacal, and even comical, through morbidly tragic, sanctions imposed by Puritan judges at Salem. However, in Calvin's defense, Calvin did not start a law school in Geneva, but would to God there had been application of the Scriptural requirement of confirming/corroborating testimony in court proceedings (*cf.* Num. 35:30; Deut. 17:6, 19:15; 1 Kings 1:14, 21:10–13; Is. 8:2; Matt. 18:16, 26:60–61; John 8:17–18; 1 Tim. 5:19; Heb. 10:28–29)!

(Geneve: Slatkine Reprints, 1970).

CONCLUSION

RELIGIOUS TOLERATION AND PLURALISM WERE NOT ON THE RADAR IN CALVIN'S DAY

The common modern criticism of Calvin's denial of ideological pluralism is historically apropos—"If Calvin ever wrote anything in favor of religious liberty, it was a typographical error" is a facetious critique, but not without a kernel of truth.[7] The legal and political scenario of Calvin's day involved upheavals deriving from the force of religion upon law, not in the thrall of the question "Should religion in public life be tolerated?" but rather "Which religion should be enforced, to the public banning of all others?" Before the sterling contribution of John Locke, religious pluralism would not come into its own.

CALVIN'S DRIVING PURPOSE WAS THE QUESTION OF HIS TIME

Calvin's purpose was not to draft a model legal code, or codify procedural due process. Rather, Calvin was driven by the power of the question, "What is the right religion?" and its ancillary corollaries: "What law is right law?" and "What government is right government?" During this era of Western history, there was no more pervasive question. Driven ever so powerfully by this and related questions, this seeker found his answers, rightly or wrongly. As to his conclusions, the world remains his jury.

---

7. As quoted by Gordon H. Clark, *Predestination* (Phillipsburg: Presbyterian and Reformed Publishing Co., 1987), p. 144.

BIBLIOGRAPHY

Berman, Harold J. "Religious Foundations of Law in the West: A Historical Perspective." *Journal of Law and Religion*, Volume 1, Number 1, Summer 1983.

Flynn, John Stephen. *The Influence of Puritanism on the Political and Religious Thought of the English*. New York: E.P. Dutton, 1920.

Haller, William. *Liberty and Reformation in the Puritan Revolution*. New York: Columbia University Press, 1955.

Pearson, A.F. Scott. *Church and State—Political Aspects of Sixteenth Century Puritanism*. Cambridge: At the University Press, 1927.

Seaver, Paul S. *Journal of Church and State*, Volume 26, Number 1, Winter 1984.

Tatham, G.B. *The Puritans in Power—A Study in the History of the English Church from 1640 to 1660*. Cambridge: At the University Press, 1913.

Margo Todd, *Christian Humanism and the Puritan Social Order* (Cambridge: Cambridge University Press, 1987.

Zaret, David. *The Heavenly Contract—Ideology and Organization in Pre-Revolutionary Puritanism*. Chicago: The University of Chicago Press, 1985.

Wilson, John F. *Pulpit in Parliament*. Princeton, University Press, 1969.

INDEX OF SCRIPTURE

ANCIENT NEAR EASTERN TEXTS

Alalakh
    38n52

Exhnunna
    38n52

Hammurabi, inscriptions of
    38n52

Kuban Stele of Rameses II
    38n52

Lipit-Ishtar
    38n52

Mentuhotep, inscriptions of
    38n52

Merneptah, tale of
    38n52

Ras Shamra
    38n52

Ur-Nammu
    38n52

Yehimilk inscription
    38n52

INDEX OF SCRIPTURE

OLD TESTAMENT

Genesis

1:24	7n27
3:15	58, 58n34
7	66
9:6	86n36
12:15	19n25
26:10	18n17, 19n23
27:11	18n19
29:27	19n22
31	38n52
38	38n52
38:24	18n17

Exodus

19	85n33
19:1	21, 22n39, 22n43, 22n44
20:1–6	85n33, 86n35
20:13	86n36, 86n37, 86n38, 88n43
20:14	86n41
21:16	87n42, 111, 111n16
21–23	23
21:23	86n36, 86n37, 86n38, 88n43
22:18	85n34
22:19	86n39
22:20	85n33

Leviticus

18	86n40
24:1–16, 23	86n35
24:10–16	86n35
24:16	86n35
24:23	86n35

Numbers

5:11–31	38n52
35:30	134

Deuteronomy

	36
5:6–10	85n33, 86n35
5:17	86n36
5:18	86n41
17:6	134
17:14–15	64
17:15	64, 65
17:20–23	86n40
18:9–11	85n34
18:15	134
19:15	134
21:18–21	38n52
22:13–21	38n52
23:29	48n10
24:16	38n52

Judges

	52
1:36	53n6

1 Samuel

8	37
8:11	38

2 Samuel

5:3	65

INDEX OF SCRIPTURE

1 Kings

1:14	134
21:10–13	134

2 Kings

14:6	38n52

1 Chronicles

11:3	65

2 Chronicles

19:6	64, 65
19:11	97
23:3	65

Job

	36

Psalms

19:7–8	23n47
119	23

Proverbs

8	101n93
8:15	101

Isaiah

1:17	38n52
2:3	22n39, 22n41
8:2	134
60:12	101
49:23	101n94

Jeremiah

1:13	134
7:6	38n52
22:13–21	38n52
31:29–30	38n52
31:31–34	52

Ezekiel

	104
14:12–20	38n52
18:10–20	38n52
20:11	23n50

Daniel

	36
6	41
6:22–23	41

Hosea

5:11	41

Amos

7	32
7:10–13	32n27, 32n28

Micah

5:5	32n26, 37

INDEX OF SCRIPTURE

NEW TESTAMENT

Matthew

17:1	134
18:16	134
20:25	98
26:60–61	134

Mark

10:42	98

Luke

12:13	98
22:25	98

John

8	86n41
8:1–12	86n41, 98
8:17–18	134
17:17	80
18:36	44n81

Acts

	103
5:29	41
7:38	23n47
17:1ff.	3
17:26–29	112
23:3	44n80
23:5	43n78, 43n79

Romans

	10
7:2	22n44
7:19	23
10:4	15
10:5	22n43
13:1	43n77
13:1–7	28, 30, 41, 44, 44n83, 45n84, 69
13:2	38n61
13:3	29n11, 40

1 Corinthians

7:37	18n16
9:1	18n20

2 Corinthians

3:6	22n42
3:7	23n46
3:14–17	23n47
13:1	134

Galatians

	21
3:10	23n49
3:19	21
4:26	22n40

Ephesians

5:31	18n16
6:1	19n25

1 Thessalonians

4:17	48n11

INDEX OF SCRIPTURE

2 Thessalonians

3:15   37

1 Timothy

2   18n16
5:8   18n16, 18n18
5:19   134

Titus

3:1   43n76

Hebrews

10:28–29   134

1 Peter

2:18   111n19

2 Peter

3:10   78n4

Revelation

20:7–15   78n4

INDEX OF SUBJECTS

absolute power, 30, 34, 35, 74
absolutism, 33
academy at Geneva, engaged Knox, 67–68
accusatory character, of the law, 24
accused parties, as guilty until proven guilty, 121
Act of Supremacy, 27, 96
Acts (Book of), Cartwright fashioning ecclesiastical government from, 103
ad fontes ("back to the original sources"), 102, 133
Adam, 23, 57–58, 59
Adam and Eve, 111
adultery, 19, 87, 87n41
"all or nothing" modality, of Sewall's approach, 113
ambiguity, of Calvin's work, 5
Ambrose, 99
American constitution, people submitting to, 75
American Puritan consensus, indicting Anabaptists, 90
American Puritan era, Samuel Sewall as the most famous judge of, 105
Ames, William, 60–62
anabaptists, 9–10, 90
Emperor Anastasius, 96n73
Andrewes, Lancelot, 83–84

Anglican Puritans, 114n26
anxiety, simplistic "solution" for, 120
Appellation to the Nobility, by John Knox, 73–74
Aquinas, Calvin differing from, 36
Archbishop of Canterbury, examined John Lambert for heresy, 127n62
Arminianism, Calvinism compared to, 7–8
Augustine, 6–7, 8, 23, 133
authorities, rebellion against as rebellion against, 39
authority
of men in Massachusetts Bay, 128
of princes, 39

bail, denied to those awaiting trial, 121
Baker, J. Wayne, 67
Baptists, statute against in Massachusetts, 89–90
barbarism, forged by war and wilderness, 120
bare law, 21, 23
Barrow, Henry, 127n62
Bartolus, 33
believers, responsibility to rebel, 74

INDEX OF SUBJECTS

Bellingham, Governor, on use of "violence" to compel confession, 126
Berman, Harold J., 104
Beza, Theodore, 54
Bible
  God gave nations his law in, 94
  John Calvin's study of, 14, 20
  John Lilburne entering the House of Commons with his, 95
  society submitting to law as laid down in, 77
  as the standard of purity, 76, 114n26
  as without error, 74
  worship of the God of as the only worship, 85, 85n33
biblical law, 18–19, 116, 117
biblical sense, church and state as distinct entities, 99
biblical teaching, on witchcraft, 119
bishopric, equating with tyranny, 63
Blackstone, William, on witchcraft, 119
Blake, on compulsory self-incrimination, 127n62
blasphemy, death penalty for, 86
blessing, of holy law excluded by depravity, 23
Bolton, Robert, 78
Boniface VIII, 96n73
Boston, Thomas, 76, 114n26
Bourne, H. R. Fox, 66
Bouwsma, 5
Bradford, William, 127
Brattle, Thomas, 124–25
"brethren," compared to "comrade" connoting Communism, 83n23
Brigomet, Guon, 10
Bucer, Martin, 34–35, 99
Bude, 20

Bullinger, 69
"Burn the witches!" as a simplistic "out," 120
burning, as a substitute for biblical stoning, 19
Burrough, George, 124n53
Burroughes, Jeremiah, 104
Burton, Henry, 80–81
Butzer, Martin, 47

Cally, William, 128n63
Calvin, John
  agreeing with Bucer, 35
  as an amalgam of the influences of his day, 133
  argued his theories before the Consistory, 75
  on checks and balances, 30–38
  on the church's influence upon the state, 27
  on the citizen's relation to government, 38–44
  compared to Paul and Augustine, 5–7
  condemned riots as sin and a crime, 14
  on the covenants of the Patriarchs, 21–22
  derived from the Bible a political and legal system, 14
  as a disciple of Jacque Lefevre d'Etaples, 10
  distinguishing King David's praises for the law from Paul's condemnation, 23
  doctrine of separation of church and state, 25
  driving purpose of, 135
  envisioning church and state as a united force, 27, 29
  fled to Geneva from his native France, 11
  influence of, 133
  integral to the reform movements, 9

INDEX OF SUBJECTS

as Jung's "the introverted thinker," 4
learning about from enemies and followers, 3–8
legal studies of, 20
legal theory of, 15–24, 132–35
letter introducing Knox, 69
maladies of, 4
maxims from, 75
not distinguishing religion from life, 45
not reforming of the law of evidence, 134
not viewing church and society as compartmentalized, 24
as oedipally ambivalent, 5
Owen and Locke as disciples of, 66
political theory of, 25–45, 132–35
political values of, 45
on the politics of civic life, 18–19
on the prosecutorial function of the law, 23–24
on rebellion, 42
rebuking civil authorities in England and Germany, 32
relation of government to God, 44–45
relation of law and the Gospel, 20–22
religious and political landscape of his day, 8–12
replying to Knox that it was unlawful to rise up in open rebellion, 69
resisting oppressive regimes, 42–43
on the right of Christians to rebel, 94n66
as a source for Knox's political theology, 69
on the source of law, 18–20
on the state as a religious entity and stabilizing force, 28
on the term "praise" as general benefit, 29
theory of church and state, 26–29
on the theory of the two kingdoms, 96n73–97n73
on the third use of the law, 17
turned to the Roman *Corpus Juris Civilis*, 19
urging moderation on sovereigns, 35
usage of the words "law" and "grace," 20
on the uses of the law, 15–17
on the virtue of "fraternal correction," 37
warning princes not to be ruled by their subjects, 36
Calvinism, 5, 7–8
Calvinist revolution, in Scotland, 68
Calvinistic Puritan revolution, in England, Wales, and Ireland, 68
Calvinistic reformation in New England, procedural law in, 105–31
Calvinistic reformers, 76, 114n26
Calvinistic schema, on the relation between church and state, 88
Calvinists, as idolaters deifying the Swiss Reformer, 3n4
Cambridge Platform, provision on heresy, 91
capital punishment, 19, 112. *See also* death penalty
carnal copulation, 87
Carrier, Martha, 124n53
Cartwright, Thomas, 76, 95–104, 114n26
Catholic bishop, in Geneva, 12
Cawdry, 80, 81

INDEX OF SUBJECTS

Ceremonial Law, in the Old Testament, 61
Chamberlain, N. H., 108, 109, 118, 129
King Charles I, 93, 95
Charnock, Stephen, 76, 114n26
Chauncy, Charles, 127
checks and balances on political power, Calvin's theory of, 30–38
Chiever, minister present at executions, 124n53
children, mortality of ascribed to witchcraft, 119
chiliasm, 48
Christ
  acting as a priest, 87n41
  alone able to keep the law, 23
  earned righteousness for all God's elect, 58
  as the end of the law, 15
  linking the divine to mankind, 52
  not known except through his disciples, 101n93
  refused the office of a Judge, 98
  returning to establish a new heaven and new earth, 78n4
Christian gospel, using as a club for torture, even death, 29
Christian state, as God's rule by God's law according to Calvin, 28
Christianity, intellectual, moral, and spiritual cleanup of institutionalized, 114n26
Christians, striving to overcome evil with goodness, 43
Christ's kingdom, founding on the teaching and power of the Spirit, 44
church
  Calvin's creation of four offices within, 12
Cartwright arguing the superiority of, 99
civil government defending the position of, 31
  defending by violence or military power, 56
  depending upon the state, 100–101
  evangelizing and making disciples of all citizens, 25
  intellectual, moral, and spiritual cleansing of, 76
  not obstructing the state, 26
  nurturing the state by producing model citizens, 25
church and state
  Calvin's theory of, 26–29
  Cartwright on the distinction of, 96–99
  Cartwright on the relation between, 99–102
  distinction of purpose for, 26
  Puritan ideology of, 95–104
Church Fathers, writings of, 8
church of Geneva, ruled by the consistory, 26
church sovereignty, eclipse of by the state, 96
citizens, 39, 72
citizen's relation to government, Calvin's theory of, 38–44
civic regulation, Luther arguing for a decentralized government, 18
civil function, of the law, 15–16
civil government, 31–32
civil magistrate, 17, 69–70, 101
clan law, in pre-monarchical Israel, 38n57
classical republican traditions, Calvin's approval of, 36
clerical abuses, preaching halting, 83
Cloppenburg, Johannes, 59–60
Cocceius, Johannes, 56–57, 58

INDEX OF SUBJECTS

cohesiveness, of the New England social order, 116–17
common enemy, fostering strong alliances, 121
commonality
   of creed and language as unique in the Massachusetts colony, 89
   of creed and language in the Massachusetts colony, 117
confessions, 125, 125n56
Congregationalist Puritan jurisprudence, in New England, 84–91
Congregationalist Puritans, embraced the Westminster Confession, 114n26
congregations, determining their ministers, 103
conscience, Sewall confessed to clear his, 114
Conscience (Ames), 60
consent of the governed, 104, 104n102
Consistory at Geneva, 26–27, 46–50, 75
conspiracy, as sin, 73
constancy, in applying law, 28
constitutional republic, as the highest form of government, 75
constitutionalist state doctrine, Beza arguing for, 54
contemporaries, of Calvin perplexed by his rigor, 29
contribution, of John Calvin cannot be ignored, 132
contrition, day of for the whole colony, 117
corporate attorney, approaching statutes, 112
Corpus Juris Civilis, as a model, 19–20
Cotton, John, on John Calvin, 3, 132

council of 20 (small council), 27
council of 60, 27
council of 200 (lower council), 27
court orders, outlandish examples of, 50
courts of equity, 95
covenant
   with Abraham, 21
   of grace, 52, 59, 92
   between a king and his subjects, 65
   of the Old and New Testaments, 22
   reward for obeying, 59
   of works, 52
Crandall, Clark, 90
creation pact, lapsed into spiritual oblivion, 58
creed and language, commonality of unique to Massachusetts, 89, 117
critics, of Sewall, 108
Cromwell, Oliver
   on "evil seducers," 90
   held Papists to be heretics and idolaters, 104n102
   law on heretics, 90–91
   Puritan hegemony ending with his Lord's Protectorate, 114n26
   subjugation of Irish Papists, 104–2
Cromwell's Protectorate of 1640–60, 76–77
crowns, throwing down before the church, 101
Currier, Martha, 123
Cusanus, 33

d'Ailly, 33
danger, of entrusting power to one or a few, 30
David, praising God's law, 23
deacons, earthly matters relegated to, 99

INDEX OF SUBJECTS

death
  Christian gospel using as a club for, 29
  examples of sentences of, 49
  fall of Adam causing the law to bring, 23
  pressing of an adult male to, 126
death penalty, 86n35. *See also* capital punishment
  for blasphemy, 86
  for homosexuality, 87, 87n40
  for kidnappers, 111
  for manslaughter, 86, 86n37
  for murder, 86, 86n36
  for perjury, 88, 88n43
  for rebellion, 88
  for stealing a man or mankind, 87, 87n42
  for witchcraft, 85
  for worshiping any other God, 85
Decalogue, 57, 59. *See also* Ten Commandments
Declaration of Liberties, denied religious freedom, 91
demarchs of Athens, applauded by Calvin, 42
demented individuals, "confessing" to being witches, 119
democracy, associating with theocracy, 31
"Denny, Reginald," 122
destruction of a community's "idols," as a direct affront to the King in France, 13
The Devil in the Shape of a Woman (Karlsen), 128
Dibble, Sarah, 128–29
Dibble, Zachary, 128–29
"dipleuric" human aspect, of God's covenant with mankind, 52
discovery phase, as a nauseating farce, 125

Disputationes Theologicae XI de Foedere Dei et Testamento veteri & novo (Cloppenburg), 59
divine law, 15, 60
divine positive right, 60
The Doctor and the Student (St. Germain), 94
doctrinae substantia, as unaltered, 22
doctrinal and spiritual matters, church having jurisdiction over, 25
doctrine of God, 22
Dordrecht Synod, 12

ecclesiastical and political powers, Cartwright's view of overlapping, 98
ecclesiastical discipline, exercised by the local congregation, 67
ecclesiocracy, having the state as an arm of the church, 28
economic strictures, 47–48
Edwards, Jonathan, designated as the last American Puritan, 77, 114n26
Eire, 56
elders, endowed with spiritual gifts, 99
election, of an assembly's ministers, 103
elective monarchy, 35
Ellis, George Edward, 113
emotional surges, of Sewall, 110
emotions, of Calvin, 5
Endecott, advocated execution, 90
English courts, utilized torture from 1540 to 1640, 126
English Presbyterian church, Presbyterian Puritans signed a petition for, 93
English Reformation, 81, 83
ephors of Sparta, applauded by Calvin, 42

INDEX OF SUBJECTS

equal before law, biological offspring of Adam as, 111
Erastes, 27–28
Eve, 111
everlasting equity, of Sewall's religious book, 112
evidentiary analysis, travesty of, 125
evidentiary standards, raising of, 120
evil, 7n27, 26, 30, 43
Ewen, 119
excommunication, 27, 46
exhortation, to Calvin as a function of the law, 17
"An Exhortation to the Bishops to Deal Brotherly with Their Brethren," 63
extraordinary offices, in Scripture, 98

fallen mankind, 57
false witness, taking away any man's life, 88, 88n43
"familiars," forms of, 118–19
families, 66, 79
family law, in pre-monarchical Israel, 38n57
Farel, William, 10–11
federal judges, attitude of many, 130n70–31n70
First Commandment, encompassing both church and state, 27
fixation hysteria *en masse*, Salem witch burning as, 120
formal Puritanism, 114–15
Formula of Concord in Article VI, "Of the Third Use of the Law," 16
fornication, punishment for, 49
France, reaction to the reformation, 11
"fraternal correction," as a virtue, 37
Frederick the Wise, 13

free state, as much better than to be under a prince, 30
free will, 7, 58

galley slave, John Knox served as, 67
Garden of Eden, 57
Pope Gelasius I, in a letter to Emperor Anastasius, 96n73
gender factor, in witch hunting, 128–29
Genesis 3:15, on the covenant of God with Adam, 58
Geneva, transformed into a constitutional republic, 75
Genevan city-state, ruled by elected bodies, 27
Genevan community, ecclesiastical and political dimensions of, 26
Genevan society, reorganized according to Calvin's vision, 12
Germany, awareness of God, 13
Gerson, 33
Gloucester, citizens prepared for an attack by demons, 121
God
  binding contract of, 91
  citizens' highest allegiance to, 41
  covenant with Abraham compared with the New Covenant of Gospels and Epistles, 21
  imputed righteousness to unrighteous sinners, 10
  intending the rule of kings to be connected with judges, 65
  law and grace derived from the will of, 22
  law in the Bible taking precedence over kings and subjects, 94
  law of as a holy monism, 45
  obligation to bless Adam, 59

INDEX OF SUBJECTS

God *(continued)*
  as the one governor of the church and state, 103
  as part of daily commerce for Puritans, 91
  promising life to all who kept his law, 23
  putting a restraint on power by means of law, 36
  raising up leaders, 41
  reigning over both church and state, 88
  relation of government to, 44–45
  responding to his creature's comportment, 57n24
  response of, determined by Adam's actions, 57
  rule of as liberty, 94
  ruling both church and state, 25
  unity of the law of, 16
God's Word, city-state under the influence of, 32–33
goldsmith from Lyon, beheaded for counterfeiting, 49
"good" mob, materialized to blame the "evil" Satan worshipers, 120
Goodman, Christopher, 42, 70–73
goodness, retained by fallen beings, 7n27
Goodwin, John, 62–63
Goodwin, Thomas, 62, 76, 114n26
Gouge, William, 79
The Governance of Princes (Aquinas), arguing for a monarchy, 36–37
governed, obliged to enter a covenant with God, 54
government official, as a servant of God, 102
governments
  relation to God, 44–45, 64
  use of, 9
grace
  Augustine on the absence of the Spirit of, 23
  covenant of, 52, 59, 92
  derived from the will of God, 22
  distinguishing law from, 20–21
  God imputed righteousness to unrighteous sinners by, 10
  as the means of salvation, 15, 21
Graham, W. Fred, 29
Granger, Thomas, 127
Greenham, Richard, 79
group hysteria, in Massachusetts Bay, 120–22
group or social hypochondria, applying to the psychology of the Bay Colony in 1692, 122n47
group paranoia, gluing together a homogeneous Nazi society, 121
guilt, of Sewall, 106

Hale, minister present at executions, 124n53
hangings, legitimacy fueled the orgy of, 124
Harmony of the Last Four Books of Moses (Calvin), 36
Harnack, 111
heaven
  invading earth, 80
  kingdom of, 77, 78n4
  living in upon earth, 78
heavenly contract, 92
Hebrew state, as a theonomic republic, 31
Henry the Eighth, 32, 96
hereditary ruling caste, infringing liberty, 30
Hesselink, I. John, 20–21
high value of human life, Sewall's view of, 113
higher law, doctrine of, 94
"highest" power, God as, 41

INDEX OF SUBJECTS

Hippocrates twins, Cartwright's analogy of, 100
holistic worldview, of Calvin, 24
Holmes, Obadiah, 89–91
holy communion, excommunication as exclusion from, 46
holy law, nature of, 23
homily, derived from the prophet Jeremiah, 110n10
homosexuality, death penalty applying to, 87, 87n40
honesty, as more valuable than prestige for Sewall, 114
Hotman, Francis, 42
Hull, John, 113
human life, Sewall's view of the value of, 110–13
humanist scholar, Calvin as, 8
humanist scholarship, 133
humiliation, of Sewall before his peers, 130
husbanding resources in times of need, Bucer on, 34–35
hypochondriacal delusions, 122n47

ideological commonality, bound Massachusetts together, 117
idolaters, magistracy, nobility and estates commanded by God to execute, 71
idolatrous rulers, failure to resist as covenantal disobedience, 72
immorality, infractions of, 49
the impenitent, remitted politically to the care of the small council, 27
"in re," of the confession of Sewall, 118–29
indentured servitude, 110–11
indictments, as equivalent to sentences, 121
influence, Calvin's expansive and extensive, 133

innovations, suspected by Sewall, 113
Institutes (Calvin), 95, 95n70–96n70
Irish Papists, Cromwell's subjugation of, 104–2
irreligious commands, of princes, 54
Israel, offer of a throne to Gideon, 35
Israelite confederacy, before the Kingdom of Saul, 34
Italian humanists, on the self-governing city-state, 33

Jacobs, George, 124n53
King James I, 93
King Jehoshaphat, 97
"Jeremiad," in Puritan parlance, 110n10
Jesus Christ. *See* Christ
Jewel, John, 76, 97
Jewell, John, 114n26
Joannis Calvini Opera Quae Supersunt Omnia (G. Baum), 20
Johnson, 17
judges, 65, 107
Judges (book of), Vermigli on, 52
judicial authority, separation of ecclesiastical from, 98
judicial law, Ames restricting to the Jews, 61–62
jurors, asked public forgiveness in Salem, 107
just war, Augustinian doctrine of, 111, 111n15

Kantian dualism, 45
Karlsen, Carol, 128
Karlstadt, 70
Kenyan youths, of Okiek, 130
kidnappers, death penalty for, 111
King Philip's War, consequences of, 120

INDEX OF SUBJECTS

kingdom of Christ, establishing, 44
kingdom of heaven, expanding on earth, 77, 78n4
Kingdon, Robert, 13
kings
  Calvin's disparagement of ungodly, 36
  chosen by the people according to Rutherford, 64
  early in the Reformation, 33
  good government as a prerogative of, 36
  guilty of felony towards God, 55
  hereditary right not consistent with liberty, 32
Knox, John, 67–74
  on bridling the fury and rage of princes, 37
  on the duty of Christians to rebel, 94n66
  on political resistance, 42
  spiritual development, 67–69
Koninck, Carolus de, 11
Kratz, Corinne A., 130

labor unions, forbidden in Geneva, 47
Lambert, John, 127n62
Larger Catechism, exposition of the Lord's Prayer, 78n4
Laud (author), 95n70–96n70
law. *See also* natural law; Puritan law; religious law
  all deriving from God, 45
  Calvin's view of the uses of, 15–17
  constancy in applying, 28
  distinguishing from grace, 20–21
  governed Geneva, 75
  as a means of religious transformation of society, 115
  as a means of salvation, 21
  needing be moral, 62
  as *nuda lex* or "bare law," 21
  as a principal concern of Reformers, 15
  restraining sin, 16
law and Gospel, continuity of, 21–22
law and grace, derived from God's will, 22
law and politics, Bible must govern, 74
law eternal, 60
law of evidence, lack of reform in, 134
law of Moses, requiring witnesses, 134
law of nature, 95, 97n73
Lectures on the Book of Judges (Bucer), 34, 35
Lefevre D'Etaples, Jacques, 10, 11
legal and political theory of John Calvin, legacy of, 132–35
legal statutes, Sewall's religious book of, 112
legal theory
  of John Calvin, 15–24
  monadic, 24
  Puritan, 92–95
  Reformation, 24
Leveret, Mr., contacted Cromwell, 90
Levitical priests, as ordinary officers, 98
Lex Rex (Rutherford), 63, 97n73
Ley, John, 79
liberty, 31, 88, 94, 110
Lilburne, John, 95
literacy, stirred by publications in the vernacular, 9
Little Council. *See* small council
livestock, mortality of ascribed to witchcraft, 119
Loci Communes (Vermigli), 52
Locke, John, 66, 67, 97n73, 135
Lord's Prayer, Farel's commentary on, 11

INDEX OF SUBJECTS

Lord's Protectorate, of Cromwell, law on heretics, 90–91
Lord's Supper, 83
Luther, Martin, 10, 18, 20, 21
Lutherans, on princes protecting Christians, 51

MacBeth, Shakespeare's three witches in, 118
Machen, J. Gresham, 8
Machiavelli, 33–34
magisterial branch of the Reformation, on civil law as a means to reform society, 15
magisterial reform, 9
magisterial Reformation political theology, Knox representing the most extreme application of, 74
magistrates
 Cartwright calling on to throw down their crowns, 100
 choosing, 31
 duty to protect people from the license of kings, 42
 duty to resist tyranny, 39
 responsibility to the "temple of God," 55–56
 subject to God's glory, 44
 subordinate resisting superiors for the Reformation's sake, 52–53
magistratus populares, Calvin arguing for, 35
mandate (*mandatum*), of Moses, 22
mankind, as evil, 7n27
manslaughter, death penalty for, 86, 86n37
Manton, Thomas, 76
the many (*plures*), holding sway (*gubernacula*), 36
"the marketplace of the soul," Sabbath as, 80
marriage, of Sewall, 108

Marsilius of Padua, 33
Massachusetts Bay Colony
 authority rested exclusively with men, 128
 basic code of law, 85n33
 as a child of England's Congregationalist Puritan sect, 84
 commonality of creed and language, 89, 117
 group hysteria in, 120–22
 legal development of, 115
 loss of the charter of, 120
 Puritan hegemony over, 114n26
 social unrest rare in, 89
 speaking against God as abominable in, 86n35
 statute against Baptists, 89–90
 structured by religious law, 115
Mather, Cotton, 109, 124n53
mature considerations, allowing liberty to be taken from others, 110
Maurer, William, 18
maxims, from Calvin, 75
McNeil, John, 30, 42
medical doctors, on diseases having supernatural origin, 119
medieval theologians, rejected by Luther, 10
meekness, spirit of ruling, 44
Melancthon, 16, 18
men
 accused of witchcraft, 128
 as offspring of God, 112
 mental degenerates, as credible sources, 119
merrymakings, Sewall fond of, 109
"minister of God," meaning of, 44
ministers
 asked public forgiveness in Salem, 107
 congregations voting for, 103
 integrity and education of Puritan, 83

men *(continued)*
  not to concurrently serve as judges, 99
  perpetuated the belief in witchcraft, 119
  Puritan limited by civil laws, 100n85
minor authorities, duties of, 34
"mobocracy," 121
mobs, in the Netherlands, 12
mock examination, of witnesses, 122–25
moderation, as a virtue rare in kings, 35
modern Western pluralism, on law as a governing entity, 24
modus administrationis, of the covenants, 22
monadic covenant, 57
monadic legal theory, 24
monarch of England, as also the head of the English state church, 96
monarchs. *See* kings
monarchy, not agreeing to all societies of men, 66
monergistic act, God's covenant as a, 52
moral and legal error, Sewall's confession proceeded from, 128
moral and legal issues, as either right or wrong to Sewall, 112
moral good, 7, 7n27
moral inflexibility, of Sewall, 113
moral law, and the law of nature as contiguous, 60–61
More, John, 83
Mosaic judicial law, 28, 32
Moses
  covenant of grace established by God, 59
  holding two titles *(munera)*, 22
  law of, 134
  placed high value upon human life, 111
  political system of, 28, 32
  prescribed no prisons and only temporary custody, 126
  as supreme judge, 98
motivation, of Sewall to recant, 107–29
Mumford, Lewis, 47
murder
  death penalty for, 86, 86n36
  by deception and poisoning, 87, 87n38
mutual admonition, providing checks and balances against arrogance, 37

natural law
  Adam responsible for conserving, 59
  Ames equating right natural, 60
  capital punishment sanctioned by, 19
  people's sovereignty under, 33
  as a phenomenon discerned by all nations, 20
natural light, law deduced from, 60
Nazi society, polarized-"us" against "them," 121
Nebuchadnezzar, as God's servant, 41
the Netherlands, reformation in, 12, 13
neurosis, of Calvin, 4
New England
  Puritans carried the torch of legal reform, 115
  Puritans on Christian reformation, 85
  social order as cohesive, 116–17
  unhampered by factionalism, 84
new mode of instruction *(nova docendi forma)*, 22

INDEX OF SUBJECTS

Newman, Samuel, 90
Noyes, Nicholas, 124n53, 125
Nuremberg, 34

obedience
   demanded by Calvin's God, 27
   release from due to unjust domination, 43
   subjects showing to God, 39
   suspending to princes, 70
Occam, 33
"Ode to the Sabbath," by John Sprint, 81–82
oeconomia, extending from Adam to Moses, 59–60
offices in Scripture, as "extraordinary" and "ordinary," 98
oikonomia, 59
Okiek youths in Kenya, tradition of, 130
Old Testament law, 32, 61
On the Right of Magistrates (Beza), 54
ordinary offices, in Scripture, 98
Owen, John, 66, 76, 114n26

Palmer, 80, 81
pamphlets, in the language of the people, 9
Papacy, overwhelmed by the power of the press, 133
paranoia, of Puritan society, 121
Parliament, 93, 95
paterfamilias, in pre-monarchical Israel, 38n57
Patrich, Ralph, 126–27
Paul, 6, 130, 134
Pearson, A.F. Scott, 100
Penot, John, 42
people
   authority and power of, 62–63
   choosing their own shepherds, 32

perjury, death penalty for, 88, 88n43
personal Puritanism, 115
Peter Martyr, supporting Plessis-Mornay, 55
Philip II of Spain, 13
physical abuse, Zachary Dibble accused of, 129
physical torture, by the judges at Salem, 128
Pope Pius IV, on John Calvin, 3, 132
placard campaign, all over Paris, 11
Plessis-Mornay, Johannes Phillipe Du, 54–56
pluralism, 14, 135
politic society, 65
political agenda, in France, 13
political authorities, must obey God, 44–45
political contract, binding both ruler and subjects, 33
political doctrine civil law, in New England, 85–88
political power, Calvin's theory of checks and balances on, 30–38
political resistance, rationale for, 42
political sovereignty, depending on the consent of the governed, 103
"political system of Moses," 28, 32
political themes, among Calvin's fellow reformers, 51–75
political theology. *See also* theology of resistance
   of Knox, 69–70, 73–74
political theory, of John Calvin, 25–45
Ponet, John, 70–73
positive divine right, as mutable and various, 60

INDEX OF SUBJECTS

power
  absolute, 30, 34, 35, 74
  to choose governors and kings, 64
  executive, 27, 37
  "highest" as God, 41
  to make kings, 66
  political, 30–38
  royal, 35, 64
  of the Spirit, 44
  unchecked as power unjustified, 30
"praise," meaning of for Calvin, 28–29
preachers, 82, 93
preaching, 13, 82–84
prelacy and monarchy, war to destroy, 92–93
pre-monarchical Israel, sources of law in, 38n57
Presbyterian Puritanism, Cartwright as the father of, 102
Presbyteries, elected ministers meeting in, 103
pressing, of an adult male to death, 126
presuppositions, of Calvin, 45
priests, 38n57, 87n41, 98
Primus, on the "keeping of the Sabbath law," 81
princes
  authority of, 39
  becoming chief judges in Germany, 32
  bridling the fury and rage of, 37
  Christ's admonition about Gentile, 98
  compelling to perform conditions and covenants, 53
  defending Christ's kingdom, 44
  free state as better than, 30
  grounds for limiting as religious, 35
  irreligious commands of, 54
  laying aside all their authority, 36
  protecting Christians, 51
  suspending obedience to, 70
  wicked, 40
printing press, 9, 133
prisoners, taking in a "just" war, 111
private property and business, regulating, 48
privilege, against self-incrimination, 125n56
probation, Adam's period of in Eden, 57
procedural law, in the Calvinistic reformation in New England, 105–31
Proctor, John, execution of, 124n53
professional infractions, trials for, 49
prophetia, 83, 83n28
prosecutorial function of the law, Calvin's view of, 23–24
Ptolemaeus of Lucca, 33
public confession, of Samuel Sewall, 106–7, 117
public humiliation, trauma of for Sewall, 130–31
public policy, five phases in Geneva, 50
public policy-making "think tank," Consistory as Geneva's, 46–47
public recantation, of Sewall, 106
"puissance," implying legal right, 38
Puritan agenda for reform, 78
Puritan covenant theology, 91–92
Puritan hegemony, over Massachusetts, 114n26
Puritan hope, 77, 79
Puritan ideology, of church and state, 95–104

INDEX OF SUBJECTS

Puritan jurisprudence, 76–84, 89–91
Puritan law, substantive, 84–89, 115–16
Puritan lawyers, evoking public opinion, 93
Puritan legal theory, 92–95
Puritan ministers, 83, 100n85
Puritan pamphlet, on divine right, 93–94
Puritan political agenda, 115
Puritan post millennial eschatology, 77–78, 78n4
Puritan reformation, 85, 115
Puritan revolution, 92
Puritan social contract, 91
Puritan social theory, Sabbath observance and, 79–82
Puritan society, degenerated into mania, 121
Puritan utopia, vision of, 78–79
Puritan vision, of a spiritual metamorphosis, 79
Puritan war with Charles, influence on Puritan legal theory, 92–95
Puritanism
  Calvin's magisterial influence extended through, 76–104
  centrality of preaching in, 82–84
  dimensions of, 114–15
  as an interdenominational movement, 114n26
  origin of, 76
  produced a mind taut with spiritual tension, 120–21
  submitting to law as laid down in the Bible, 77
Puritanism and Liberty (A. S. P. Woodhouse), 63n50
Puritans
  Anglican, 114n26
  authority built around a Calvinistic model of the church-state, 93
  Congregationalist, 114n26
  Deuteronomic vision of, 80
  establishing kingdom of heaven on earth, 77
  God's binding contract for, 91
  hardened by King Philip's War, 120
  hatred of sexual deviation, 87n39
  laws forcing society to listen to their preaching, 84
  in New England, 85, 115
  as preachers before anything else, 82
  Separatist, 76n1, 114n26
  speaking against God as abominable, 86n35

radical branches, of the Reformation, 9
rebellion
  against authorities as against God himself, 39
  death penalty for, 88
  John Calvin on, 42, 69
  against the magistrate as striving after anarchy, 43
  Philip II of Spain suppressing in the Netherlands, 13
recantation, of Samuel Sewall, 106–7
reciprocity, denying, 27
Reformation
  accelerating the growth of political theories, 33
  in all things sought by the Puritans, 77
  began at the local level, 33
  consensus on error having no rights, 74
  contending with proponents of absolutism, 33

INDEX OF SUBJECTS

Reformation *(continued)*
  dismantled the bishopric in Geneva, 12
  ignited in the Netherlands, 12
  legal theory of, 24
  printing press as the weapon of, 9
  reached an epic dimension after 1530, 11
  Rutherford on the quest for, 64–65
  in Scotland, 70–73
The Reformed Doctrine of Predestination (Boetnner), 8
Reformed society, of Calvin, 25
Reformed theologians, 8
Reformers, arguing against absolute power, 74
religiosity, fundamental to Calvin's Reformed society, 25
religious consensus, yielded a social, legal, and political consensus, 75
religious law, Sewall's perception of, 114–17
religious people, relationship with magistrates, 55
religious pluralism, 135
religious republic, envisioned by Calvin, 28
religious statute book, Sewall finding the one "correct" interpretation, 112
religious toleration, in Calvin's day, 14, 135
Renaissance humanist scholar, Calvin as, 133
representative democracy, 32
republic, 31
Republica Romana, Italian humanists wanting to restore, 34
revolution, Calvin not advancing an argument for, 41
rewards and punishments, 28

rhetoric, humanist traditions revived the art of, 9
rhetorical superiority, of Calvin, 5
Richardson, Samuel, 99–100
right natural divine law, 60
rigidity, of Sewall, 109
riots, throughout France, 13
Roman Catholic doctrine, of the "two swords," 96n73
the Roman tribunes, applauded by Calvin, 42
royal power, 35, 64
rule of evidence, 134
"rule of principal persons," Calvin's reference to, 30
rulers
  appointed by the providence of God, 41
  authority from God, 39
  covenant with God according to Mornay, 54
  duty to enforce the law of God in their domains, 72
  obeying the commands of God, 102
  political contract with subjects, 33
  unjust, 39–40
Rutherford, Samuel
  on a politic society as voluntary, 65
  on political resistance, 42
  power to make kings coming from God, 66
  on the quest for Reformation, 64–65
  on resistance to civil government, 63
  A. S. P. Woodhouse on, 63–66
  wrote *Lex Rex*, 97n73

Sabbatarianism, 79
Sabbath, 47, 60, 79–82
sacral law, in pre-monarchical Israel, 38n57

INDEX OF SUBJECTS

sacred writings, as a source of law, 115–16
Sacrosancta regum majestas (Maxwell), 63
Salem witch trials, 105–31
salvation, 15, 21
Samuel, 37–38, 97
sanctification, by word and prayer, 80
sanctions, examples of, 49–50
Satan, 7n27, 9–10, 120
Scholastic theologians, on moral good, 7n27
school system, in Massachusetts, 89
Scotland, 68, 70–73
Scottish nobility, as the "congregation of Christ," 73
scriptural requirements, on testimony in court proceedings, 134
Scripture
  as the only source of religious authority, 10, 133
  reading without interpretative comment scorned, 83
  sense of the superiority of, 13
  translated into the language of the people, 9
secular authorities, Thomism requiring submission to, 41
"secular" law, 24
secularism, 14
secularists, modern, 45
self-governing city-state authorities, 34
self-incrimination, 125n56, 126, 127n62
Selinger, Susanne, 4–5
"The Selling of Joseph-A Memorial" (Sewall), 110
Seneca, Calvin's commentary on, 8
sentences of death, examples of, 49

Separatist Puritans, 76n1, 114n26
Sewall, Betty, 109
Sewall, Joseph, whipping of, 109
Sewall, Samuel
  comparing buying and selling a horse with buying slaves, 112
  critics and character of, 108
  crossed a line into superstition, 119
  displayed great compassion for John Hull, 113
  epitaph of, 113–14
  estranged by what he done in the Salem witch trials, 117
  experienced emotional surges, 110
  perception of religious law, 114–17
  present at executions, 124n53
  psychological, moral, and religious underpinnings, 108–14
  public confession in the witch trials, 106–7
  recanting of, 106, 107–29
  role of in the Salem witch trials, 105–31
  temperament of, 109–10
  view of the value of human life, 110–13
  written recantation of, 106–7
Sibbes, Richard, 92
"siblings," humankind consisting of, 111
Simns, present at executions, 124n53
sin, as a guarantee of divine punishment, 73
"sins," recasting, 130
slavery, 110, 111
slaves, converted to Christ remaining slaves, 111n19
small council, possessed executive power to punish impenitents, 27, 37

161

INDEX OF SUBJECTS

Smith, Morton, on Arminianism, 7
social contract, derived from mutual assent, 91
social debts, public confession of by Okiek youths in Kenya, 130
social dysfunction, 108
social infractions, examples of, 48–49
social order, established by Puritan law, 88–89
social stigma, of excommunication, 46
social theory, 50, 78, 79–82
social unrest, as rare in the Bay Colony, 89, 116
societies, moving from one religion to another, 14
sociopolitical contract, 53
"sola scriptura," fueled Calvin's epistemology, 133
sons of Zebedee's wife, Christ's admonition to, 98
"sound doctrine," 31–32
source of law, Calvin's view on, 18–20
sovereignty of the people, theorists arguing for, 33
"spark of divinity," 7
speaking against God, as abominable, 86n35
Special Court of Oyer and Terminer, 124n53
spectral evidence, 119–20, 124n53, 134
spectres, 124
spiritual aspect, of God's covenant with mankind, 52
spiritual resurgence, calling an "apostatizing" colony to, 110n10
spiritualists, viewed the state as an arm of Satan, 9–10

Sprint, John, "Ode to the Sabbath," 81–82
Sproul, R. C., 8
Spurgeon, Charles Haddon, 5
St. Germain, Christopher, 94–95
state
  as better ruled by elected officials, 30
  governed by elected representatives as the highest good, 31
  healthy only while the church is healthy, 99
  maintaining domestic tranquility, 25, 100
  needing the church, 101
  setting the stage for the church, 26
state and church, as mutually religious, 26
status quo, represented by the monarchy and the prelacy, 93
statutory law, forbade witchcraft, 119
"stealing," slave trading as, 111
stealing a man or mankind, death penalty for, 87, 87n42
steward of general doctrine, Moses as, 22
stocks, sentences for hours in, 49
Storms, Sam, 7–8
Stoughton, 121
Chief-Justice Stoughton, 128, 128n63
Stoughton, 128n63
Strassbourg, as and self-governing, 34
subjects
  acquainted with higher law, 94
  Calvin warning princes not be ruled by, 36
  King Charles I on the disaffection of his, 93
  covenant between a king and, 65

INDEX OF SUBJECTS

rebelling if magistrates choose to rebel, 56
responsible for their own obedience, 38–39
responsible for their own person and body, 55
rulers political contract with, 33
submission, as conspiracy, 73
substantive Puritan law, 84–88, 115–16
suicide, 94
Sunday, as a day of rest by Genevan law, 47
superstitions, tragic, 118–20
Supremacy Act, 27, 96
Synod of Dordrecht, 12

Table of God's Law, envisioned by Beza, 54
Tawney, R. H., 47
teleology, of Puritan jurisprudence, 77–84
temporal matters, state having jurisdiction over, 25
Ten Commandments. *See also* Decalogue
as "bare law," 23
theocracies, both the church and state as, 102
theocracy
associating with democracy, 31
every nation becoming a Christian, 78n4
fundamental to Calvin's Reformed society, 25
God ruling the state and church, 28
Puritan hope for universal, 77
theological blame shifting, 128–29
theology of resistance. *See also* political theology
of Vermigli, 52
theonomy, 25, 28
third use the law, functions of, 16–17

Thomism, requiring submission to secular authorities, 41
Three Estates (lower magistrates), 42
tinsmiths, petitioned the Consistory, 48
tombstone inscription, of Sewall, 113
Toon, Peter, 66
torture, extracting confessions, 125–28
treason, requiring two witnesses, 127n62
tree of knowledge, representing Adam's temptation, 57
trials, majority ended in a fine or imprisonment, 49
truth, as the first casualty of war, 92
Turretin, Francis, 51
tutelary use, of the law, 15
twins of Hippocrates, 100
"two kingdoms" doctrine, of Calvin, 96
"two swords," Roman Catholic doctrine of, 96n73
tyranny
equating the bishopric with, 63
likely whenever power is in the hands of the few, 30
magistrates resisting, 39, 94n66
usurping the supreme power by force, 37

Udall, John, 128n62
ungodly, convicting of guilt, 43
universal God, governing through universal law, 24
universal prosperity, under theocratic rule, 78n4
universal theocracy, Puritan hope for, 77
unjust domination, release from obedience to, 43

INDEX OF SUBJECTS

unjust rulers, viewed as a judgment from God, 39–40
unlawfulness, Sewall leaving the "slavery" of, 116
upheavals, deriving from the force of religion upon law, 14
usury, Calvin on, 47, 48

van Ruler, Arnold, 27
Vermigli, Peter Martyr, 52–53
Vindiciae contra turannos (Plessis-Mornay), 54
Vingle, Pierre de, 11
Viret, 69
voting, as a right requiring good standing within the church, 26

Walker, George, 80, 91
"walking with God," as a spiritual ideal, 78
wealth, persons with oppressing the general body, 36
Wendell, 109
Wesley, John, on witchcraft, 119
Westminster Confession of Faith, 76, 78n4, 114n26
"What is the true religion?" as the question driving Calvin, 14, 135
Whitaker, William, 83
Whitelam, Keith W., 38n57
Whitgift, unified view of church and state, 96
wicked prince, visited upon the governed as punishment for their sins, 40

Wiggenton, 127n62, 128n62
Wigglesworth, Michael, 129–30
Willard, John, 124n53
Willard, Simon, 122–23
Winslow, 109–10
witch hunting, gender dimension of, 128
witch trials, 105–31
witchcraft, 85n34–86n34, 119, 129
Witchcraft and Demonianism (Ewen), 119
witches, putting to death, 85
witnesses, mock examination of, 122–25
Wittenberg Movement, 13
woman taken in adultery, Christ's response to, 98
women
  having "teats" for imps or animal "familiars," 118
  as offspring of God, 112
Woodhouse, A. S. P., 60, 63–66
word of God, 33, 101
worship of the God of the Bible, 85, 85n33
worshiping any other God, death penalty for, 85

Yahweh, tolerating no other gods, 27
Yale, founding of, 115n26

Zaret, David, 91–92
Zwingli, 10

www.ingramcontent.com/pod-product-compliance
Lightning Source LLC
Chambersburg PA
CBHW060819190426
43197CB00038B/2128